# Whatever Else Happened to the Egyptians?

## From the Revolution to the Age of Globalization

## Galal Amin

Translated by David Wilmsen
Illustrations by Samir Abd al-Ghani

The American University in Cairo Press
Cairo • New York

English translation copyright © 2004 by
The American University in Cairo Press
113 Sharia Kasr el Aini, Cairo, Egypt
420 Fifth Avenue, New York, NY 10018
www.aucpress.com

Second printing 2004

Copyright © 2003 by Galal Amin
First published in Arabic in 2003 as *'Asr al-gamahir al-ghafira 1952–2002*
Protected under the Berne Convention

Dar el Kutub No. 7688/03
ISBN 977 424 819 8

Printed in Egypt

# Contents

# Introduction

This book describes aspects of the development of Egyptian society over the last fifty years, covering the second half of the twentieth century. It could therefore be considered as a continuation of what I had begun in *Whatever Happened to the Egyptians* (Cairo: The American University in Cairo Press, 2000), since it deals with subjects that were not addressed in that book. However there is another important difference: whereas the dominant theme of the first book was one of social mobility, and the effect that a changing class structure in Egypt had on social phenomena, this book focuses on the effects of population size, or, rather, the growth in absolute terms of the "influential" or "effective" part of the population, regard-

1

less of changes in the size of one class relative to another. It is my belief that the effects of the increase in absolute size of the influential segments of the population are of no less importance than the effects of the changes wrought by the growth in relative terms of one class vis à vis another.

This book is by no means exhaustive: I have addressed just some of the social and economic factors, however important, that have been affected by this absolute growth, among them culture and the economy, journalism, television, dress, and romance. Doubtless there are many more aspects of social life, no less important than those mentioned here, that have also been affected by the emergence of what I refer to throughout this book as a "mass society."

In chapter one I attempt to explain the importance of the phenomenon of a mass society and its relationship to the emergence of another world phenomenon, which may be called "the American Era," on the assumption that there is a strong link between so-called Americanization and the emergence of a mass society. In chapter two, I propose that in the combination of these two phenomena, as they relate to Egypt, may lie the real significance of the July Revolution of 1952. In subsequent chapters I examine one aspect after another of Egypt's social life as it has been affected by these two phenomena.

Galal Amin
Cairo, October 2002

# 1

## The Age of the Mass Society

It was about fifty years ago that I first boarded an airplane. I still recall how passengers comported themselves in those days. We were "airline passengers," a rare breed of earth denizen, aristocrats in every sense of the word, and we were treated as such by airline staff, stewardesses, and ticket agents alike.

Everything was so much cheaper then than it is now, yet the few pounds of the price of an airline ticket were well beyond the means of most of the world's population, who for that reason were resigned to a life in their local cities or towns, destined never to leave them. If they were lucky, they could probably travel from one place to another by train, the mode of long-distance transport that was far more common in those days than the airplane.

How things had changed when, many years later, I found myself standing in a long line waiting to board a flight to the Gulf! Most of the people in line with me were Egyptian laborers, who, instead of being dressed like me in shirt and pants, were all wearing *gallabiyas*—pressed and clean *gallabiyas*, to be sure, as befits the status of an air trip—but it was clear from their dress that they were of modest means, and were heading to the Gulf to look for work. What's more, many of them could neither read nor write, as evinced by their requests for help in filling out landing cards.

The attitudes of the airline employees had changed accordingly. We the passengers were no longer a world aristocracy; we had become the teeming masses, swarming daily through airports and onto planes. Now we were millions, instead of mere hundreds, the flight attendants handing out our mess trays without so much as a smile, and without the deference of days past.

As I recall how flying has changed over the past fifty years, another impression forces itself on me. Far fewer than fifty years ago I had the chance for the second time in my life to view *La Pieta*, Michelangelo's famous sculpture housed in St. Peter's Basilica in Rome, a magnificent work, depicting the Virgin Mary cradling the body of Christ after his removal from the cross. When I first saw it in 1959, I was able to approach from within a step or two and examine it at close range. A few years ago, I was in Rome again, and approached to take another look at the statue, only to find that a protective barrier had been installed in front of it to keep back the throngs of visitors. I could not come any closer than ten or twenty meters, and found myself just one of hundreds of tourists descending on the same spot at the same time to have a look. I experienced the same feelings I had had while standing in line for the plane to the Gulf: forty or fifty years ago I had been the member of a world aristocracy; now I was one of the masses, indistinguishable from the pack, no longer privy to a pleasure or sensation not shared by countless others.

This is at once a sorrowful yet joyful phenomenon. As much as the elite have declined and been taught a lesson in humility, so have the masses been liberated and attained to rights previously denied them. This has been the true gain and lynchpin of world progress over the past fifty years. Perhaps we are not as happy or as refined as we were fifty years ago, but it is certain that what was once limited to the few is now in the hands of the many. This appears to be the main defense of modern technology. It is doubtful that it has made us happier or more refined; it has simply made us more.

It was Winston Churchill, whose name is inextricably linked with the Allied victory in the Second World War, who described the twentieth century, the last third of which he did not live to see, as "that dreadful century!" Nevertheless, no matter what we may have to say about its appalling cruelty—two world wars, deep economic crises, merciless dictatorial regimes, two atomic bombs, and so on—this century possesses at least one merit, one thing in which it outstrips all the centuries that came before it, and in which it will probably surpass those that come after it too: it has granted the gift of life to the greatest number of people.

The twentieth century received from the preceding century one-and-a-half billion people; it bequeaths to the twenty-first, six billion. In other words, the number of the world's inhabitants has increased four times during the century. Compare that number with the situation before the twentieth century. Two-and-a-half centuries ago the world's population was less than the current population of India; even in 1850, only a century-and-a-half ago, the entire population of the world was less than that of China today.

The average life expectancy for a child born in 1900 was about fifty years in the most developed and affluent countries and not more than twenty-five in the poorest. Now it has approached eighty in the former and sixty-five in the latter. It might be asked: "What good is a longer life if it doesn't also become better? Look at the number of poor and hungry people in the world today. There are also billions of these." This, though true, does the twentieth century some injustice. For it is also true that never, over the course of its long history, has humanity witnessed as great a proportion of its numbers enjoying the finer things of life as it has done in the twentieth century, particularly during the past fifty years. Yes, the proportion of people suffering from malnutrition today amounts to as much as one third of the entire world population, but the corresponding figure of fifty years ago was closer to one half. Similar observations can be made about other human needs such as adequate clothing and shelter, education and mass transit, and many other sources of comfort that were completely unknown a half-century ago in large parts of the world—amenities such as electric lights, the telephone, cinema, radio, television, and so on.

Thus, the past fifty years have not only brought about a huge increase in the size of the world population (from 2.5 billion in 1950 to six billion in 2000), they have also seen an increase in that proportion of people rising above mere subsistence to enjoy the fruits of modern technology, and who must therefore be taken into greater account from a political point of view.

The emergence of the phenomenon of a "mass society" is therefore not merely the result of an increase in population size. A country's population may be rising at a rapid rate while the majority of people remain invisible, unable to make their presence felt or their wishes known, mainly because of their low purchasing power. The vital issue here is not the absolute, but rather the "effective" size of the population, that is, that part of the populace that influences and shapes the pattern of a country's life. What has happened in Egypt over the past fifty years, and indeed in the world as a whole, is that both figures have risen sharply—the absolute size of the population as well as its effective size—and this explosion on two fronts has led to what I refer to as the phenomenon of a "mass society."

\* \* \*

This phenomenon is not difficult to explain. After the end of the Second World War, the concept of the "welfare state" spread throughout the more affluent industrialized countries of the West. States assumed responsibilities to which they had previously only lent a token hand, or which they had simply not assumed at all. They began to provide all manner of basic services such as healthcare, education, and various forms of social insurance, at prices that were within the reach of most people, and in the spirit of a serious obligation from the state to its citizens. This allowed large sections of previously marginalized sections of the population to rise to the surface of society and make their presence felt.

The adoption of socialism had a similar effect in Russia after the First World War, but the idea of the welfare state did not spread to the rest of Eastern Europe until it came under Soviet control after the Second World War. The Soviet model created resounding echoes in many countries of the Third World, especially after the decisive military victory of the Soviet Union in the Second World War. After that, one country after another, from China in the east to Cuba in the west, began to adopt Soviet economic and social measures that led to a significant increase in the proportion of their citizens living above subsistence level.

There was also, of course, the wave of "economic development" that spread after 1945 in those countries that were referred to at the time as "underdeveloped." This was the result of the interaction of a number of factors, the most important of which was these countries' liberation from

8

European colonialism, the outbreak of the Cold War, and the ensuing rivalry between socialist and capitalist camps for influence over these newly-independent states. "Economic development" very often proved to be little more than the exchange of one form of colonialism for another, whether the new form was of the "capitalist" or "socialist" variety. But whatever the case may be, the development projects coincided with a widening of the circle of people enjoying a better life, or at least rising above subsistence. If we add all this to the increase in the absolute size of the population brought about by the large reduction in death rates over the last fifty years, one has good reason to call these fifty years the "Age of the Mass Society."

One important observation should be added, however, which concerns the link between the emergence of a mass society and technological advancement. For, to contend that the emergence of the phenomenon of a mass society was associated with the rise of the welfare state in some countries, the introduction of socialism in others, and the impact of economic development in yet another group of countries, while true, refers merely to the influence of ideas and policies that could not possibly have been implemented had they not been backed by some progress in productive capacity. However radical the socialist principles in question, and however strong the desire to bring the fruits of development to the masses, neither could have come about without the necessary progress in the means of production. No wonder that socialist movements and ideas met with so little practical success throughout the nineteenth century.

If this is the case, one must expect to see a close relationship between the degree of technological progress achieved and the degree of advancement of the mass society. This close relationship explains how, for example, the Scandinavian countries have been much more successful than the Soviet Union, for all its slogans, in raising the level of consumption of essential goods and services for a large proportion of their population. It also explains the great variety in the degrees of success achieved by various Third World countries in realizing the same goal, a variety resulting not from different levels of radical ideology, but from the extent of their success in developing their productive power.

But most importantly for our purposes, this may also shed light on the unique experience of the United States. The United States emerged from the Second World War with indisputably the strongest economy and highest standard of living in the world. It had made greater progress than any other country toward bringing the fruits of modern technology to within the reach of the great majority of the population. Indeed, it is possible to say that before the start of the Second World War the United States was the only country in which a mass society had appeared.

The United States was well prepared for this development by a number of factors, the most important of which was its vast market and rich natural resources. These two factors enabled the United States to surpass other countries in developing the means of mass production, and led the United States to become the first country to enter what the American economic historian Walt Rostow has called the "Stage of High Mass Consumption." This was to be the final stage of Rostow's famous "Stages of Growth," or rather the "last stop" in the long path of development that all countries were assumed to take. Rostow took the mass consumption of such durable goods as private cars, refrigerators, televisions, telephones, vacuum cleaners, and air conditioners, as symbols of this stage. Many of these goods had become available to the masses in the United States before the Second World War, but began to spread to other industrial nations after the end of the war and then even to penetrate socialist and Third World countries (within the limits imposed by the degree of economic development of each country), such that it became possible to speak of the beginning of the age of mass society in these as well.

The conjunction of these two remarkable phenomena, the emergence of a mass society and the dawn of what may be called the "American Age," cannot have been a sheer coincidence, and can be explained as follows. The United States emerged from the Second World War as the country with the most advanced economy as well as the greatest military power. True, the Soviet Union came a close second when it acquired the atomic bomb, competed with the United States in space exploration, and clawed out a few footholds and bases of operation in Latin America, the

11

Middle East, Southeast Asia, and Africa, but America remained indisputably the biggest economic, military, and political power in the world. Eventually the justifications for calling the era the "American Age" increased as the economic, political, and military weaknesses of the Soviet Union became manifest, until the final victory of the United States was achieved with the break-up of the Soviet Union and the fall of the Berlin Wall in 1989.

American economic, political, and military supremacy coincided with an intense wave of American cultural influence that flooded the world in the shape of Hollywood films and American TV series, American-style food and drink, of which McDonald's hamburgers and Coca-Cola were only the most potent symbols, the spread of American styles of clothing, such as blue jeans and the preference for casual dress over more formal attire, not to mention a great variety of means of entertainment and ways of spending leisure time.

All this has often been criticized as being a cultural invasion in which a great variety of old and precious cultures were overwhelmed by a culture that was not necessarily superior but backed by immense economic and military power. This is no doubt partly true, but it is not perhaps the most important aspect of the truth. For it is also possible to view the spread of the American lifestyle as not simply the invasion of one particular culture by another, but also as a natural outcome of the desires of ordinary men and women. This is perhaps the true explanation for the remarkable worldwide triumph of the American lifestyle

12

over all others, including the European way of life at the height of European power. The explanation cannot simply be one of economic and social vigor or a particular American skill at propagandizing, but more that the American lifestyle grants ordinary people an easy material life and caters to their tastes.

For in all of America itself the true sovereigns are the simple people of the street, possessing a limited culture and education, and endowed with average intelligence and modest ambitions. They enjoy reading simple, uncomplicated fiction or watching crime films. They like to travel and visit such places such as the Louvre Museum and the Egyptian pyramids, but have little patience for history. They take a child-like pleasure in large automobiles, and readily accept the veracity of what they hear through the television or read in the newspapers.

This average person in fact represents most of the world's population, and the American variety of Western civilization, more than any other, has succeeded in satisfying their demands. What allowed the United States to accomplish this first was its unlimited wealth in resources and the extent of its market. The sheer size of its market gave the United States the opportunity to develop methods of organization based on a high degree of specialization and division of labor, while its vast natural resources allowed it to bring a great variety of goods and services within the reach of the masses. But these were the very factors that gave the American lifestyle some of its less appealing distinguishing characteristics: a very high degree of uniformity in behavior and attitude, the spread of fads, consumers on the whole obedient to the blandishments of advertising, and the veneration accorded to media stars of every kind.

Consider the millions of dollars that can be spent on a beautiful actress, even if she cannot act, or on a television announcer, even if she or he is of ordinary intelligence. Producers can quickly recoup their costs if they are spent in such a way as to guarantee the successful marketing of a film or program in the United States alone. All that's needed is a wide-ranging publicity campaign, which, by itself, would not guarantee a good return in a smaller market. The result must be a dominant culture that appeals to the taste of the common person, while high culture fades into an embarrassed silence for its lack of a similar patronage.

Such a culture must forever pamper and flatter the ordinary man and woman and play to their vanity. If a child can write his name, he is precocious; if he can pronounce it, he is deemed eloquent. The highest praise is reserved for game show contestants—housewives who win refrigerators and vacuum cleaners—the host never failing to praise the beauty of the homeliest one. The crucial thing is to please everyone, since the most successful programs are those viewed by the largest number of people, and it is precisely those viewers who buy up refrigerators and vacuum cleaners, the manufacturers of which underwrite the game shows in the first place. If American television is obliged for one reason or another to air serious public service programs, it broadcasts them after midnight or in the wee hours of the morning when most of the American public is asleep, since such programs appeal only to a small number of viewers who are not in any case the most in thrall to the accumulation of consumer goods.

It should come as no surprise, then, that those most critical of the American way of life are intellectuals, while simple folk, especially their young, tend to welcome it with open arms. European countries, for all their insistence on the preservation of high culture, have been unable to resist the allure of the American cultural invasion. Year by year, serious European television programs are being replaced by American entertainment, and European journalism is following the example of the American press in its reliance on sensationalism. European restaurants and coffee houses are abandoning their characteristically comfortable chairs and leisurely service for user-unfriendly seating and self-service. Even the Soviet Union, after decades of isolation, could not hold back its youth's fascination for and imitation of the American lifestyle. We live apparently, not in the age of capitalism or socialism, but in the age of the masses, of the average man and woman whose wants and aspirations have come closest to fulfillment through sheer American ingenuity and know-how.

It goes without saying that this is not necessarily a happy outcome, except in purely quantitative terms. Human progress cannot be judged merely by the proportion of its population able to acquire the desired goods and services. This is undoubtedly the economist's favorite way of measuring progress, but it is by no means the only one. Ever since Adam Smith's discussion more than two hundred years ago of the advantages of a wide market and large-scale production, which allow the firm to reap the benefits of the division of labor and increased productivity, economists cannot praise enough the advantages of economies of scale. But while large-scale production may be good for the economy, it is not necessarily beneficial to high culture. Production on a large scale requires a large demand, and in the realm of culture that may imply deterioration rather than improvement, since a more sophisticated culture is by definition that which is demanded by the few.

In this may lie one of the great blessings, but also one of the curses, of the American experience of the last two hundred years. For its great wealth in natural resources has allowed the United States to both absorb a large population, making it by the mid-twentieth century one of the four most populous countries in the world, and to achieve a high rate of income growth, making it at the same time the country with the highest per capita income. The combination of a high per capita income and a large population implies, in the economist's language, a wide market; and this large market must have been one of the most important factors behind the stunning technological progress achieved by the United States. This economic blessing was accompanied by a curse in the field of culture, for it was that very size of the market that made it immensely profitable to produce a lowbrow culture, one which appeals to the lowest common denominator of cultural likes and dislikes.

It could also be argued that a large population with a high income must also mean a large market for the more sophisticated and finer products of that culture, for doesn't a large, high-income population give rise to a larger number of educated consumers than there would be in a country with a smaller population and a lower average income? That is of course true, but the important thing here is not absolute, but relative size. The kind of culture that will ultimately prevail must be that which is demanded by the greatest portion of the population.

One example from Egypt may be given to illustrate this point. In the years before and just after the Second World War there were in Egypt two highly sophisticated cultural magazines, *al-Risala* and *al-Thaqafa*. Neither of them had a distribution of more than two thousand, but they had a great influence on the cultural life not only of Egypt but of the entire Arab world. Before the war, neither magazine was discouraged by economic problems arising from low circulation, but this changed radically after the end of the war, when the two journals began to suffer growing losses, and to complain of rising printing costs. Of course, the readership had not actually declined; quite the contrary, the number of readers naturally grew with the increase in population and the number of educated people. The problem lay not with the absolute number of readers of *al-Risala* and *al-Thaqafa*, but with their relative numbers compared to the rest of the population. For as the number of readers of these two sophisticated journals was increasing, the proportion of the total readership devoted to other types of journals, which pandered to inferior tastes, was also growing. Thus as costs rose for everyone, those magazines with wider audiences were better able to withstand these higher costs, and as a result compete with higher quality magazines, not just in the realms of printing and distribution, but also in attracting the necessary writers and editors. Inevitably, just as bad money drives out good, so the low-quality magazines drove out the good ones, and *al-Risala* and *al-Thaqafa* closed down, while magazines and newspapers like *Akhbar al-Yawm*[1] grew and flourished.

The well-known Egyptian Marxist economist Samir Amin once wrote that "capitalism is the negation of culture," a statement that could be regarded, in the light of what has just been said, as containing some truth, but certainly not the whole truth.

For to the extent that "culture" refers to that which distinguishes one human community or society from another, capitalism does contribute to its weakening by spreading the same pattern of living across nations. For example, the spread of jeans and T-shirts across the world, replacing the great variety of dress in one country after another, could be regarded as the invasion of one culture by another, but it can also be seen as an act of "negation" of culture, since it does make one culture less distinguishable from another with respect to dress. The same observation can be made of fast food, which scarcely requires cooking or utensils, comfortable seating arrangements, or conversation, all of which are associated with more traditional types of cuisine, which do denote cultural differentiation. Here again, this is not merely an invasion of one culture by another but may more accurately be described as the very negation of culture; in other words, what we appear to observe is not the replacement of one kind of cooking by another, but the abandonment of cooking altogether. And what is involved here is not exactly "capitalism," but rather the great extent of the market combined with mass production. Such a scenario could as well take place under a "socialist" regime, where the means of production are publicly owned and production and consumption are planned by a central authority, as it could under a capitalist system. What "negates culture," it seems, is not capitalism but rather the spread of the mass society.

# 2

---

# The July Revolution and the Age of the Mass Society

In the three or four years before the July Revolution of 1952, a general feeling spread among Egyptians that something momentous was about to happen. They were ruled by a corrupt king, news of whose exploits with women and feats at gambling reached them every day. In 1948, the Egyptian army along with six other Arab armies suffered an ignominious defeat in Palestine that was followed by the announcement of the establishment of the state of Israel. After that, one Egyptian government followed another in quick succession, each one more corrupt than the one before. Income disparities were growing rapidly as was the population, without there appearing to be any signs that the economic policymakers had taken

account of either (assuming there was any economic policy at all). All the important political positions and social
privileges were monopolized by a very small proportion of
the population, with insurmountable barriers preventing
some 70 or 80 percent of the population from assuming
any role in public life, and reducing most of them to a
standard of living barely above subsistence level.

Little wonder then that the Egyptians greeted the news
of the revolution of July 23, 1952 with such joy, the
majority of them regarding the event as something completely natural and necessary. We were admittedly surprised that those initiating the movement were army
officers, but then we told ourselves, "And why not? Are
they not Egyptians like us, who see and share our discontent? And in any case who but they could have taken such
a bold and decisive step?"

Not only was the revolution perceived as inevitable, but
it was clear to Egyptians what the revolution needed to
accomplish, and this was precisely what was announced as
the famous "Six Principles of the Revolution": an end to
colonialism and its agents, an end to feudalism, the elimi-
nation of the domination of government by the owners of
capital, the establishment of a strong national army, social
justice, and the establishment of a genuinely democratic
system of government.

All of this seemed self-evident and beyond dispute.
Where disagreement arose, however, was over the precise
detail of how these goals could be fulfilled. For example, in
the realm of domestic policy, were the army troops to

return to their barracks once they had performed their great mission, their only domestic role being to guarantee fair elections? Or were the officers to remain in government? In foreign policy, what would happen now that Egypt had succeeded in ridding itself of British colonial occupation? Would it ally itself to the American or Soviet camp, or remain neutral? In regional policy, should Egypt aim at uniting with the Sudan, join a greater Arab unity, or try to forge a front of African or Islamic states? With the stance toward Israel, should we accept the present reality and make peace, head straight into war, or wait until we have a strong army and then make war? In economic policy, development is no doubt important, but this comes in many forms and guises. So, should we concentrate on agriculture, on industry, or strike a balance between the two? Should we try to be self-sufficient or accept foreign aid? Should we rely mainly on the private or the public sector? In industrial policy should the priority be given to light or heavy industry? To capital-intensive or labor-intensive modes of production? In the field of social justice, to what extent should we ease class disparities? Should we implement Soviet- or Chinese-style communism? Or is the implementation of a progressive income tax without the abolishment of private property an adequate method of income redistribution?

In this chapter I will maintain that what ultimately determined the decisions of the leaders of the revolution and their successors over the past fifty years, on all of these issues, was not an ideological bias or personal preference on the part of a particular leader or clique of officers; rather it was the nature of the international arena and the changes that it went through that defined their choices. This was not readily apparent to us at the beginning of the period in question, but it has become clearer since then. What I have in mind particularly are the two dominant themes of the previous chapter, namely the rise of the so-called American Age and the emergence of a mass society. Let us now try to discover the way in which these two phenomena may have affected the course of the July Revolution.

In the last chapter, I sought to show how the end of the Second World War inaugurated an age in which large new segments of society were raised above bare subsistence and began to enjoy many of the fruits of modern technology that had previously been denied to them. This gave them the ability to affect political decisions, thereby changing the country's pre-war social and political landscape to a remarkable degree. I have observed that this change took place in the East as well as in the West, in the underdeveloped South as well as the economically developed North, although to very different degrees of course, and it is impossible to imagine how Egyptian society could have veered from the path taken by the rest of the world.

Gamal 'Abd al-Nasser would often describe Egyptian society before the 1952 revolution as the "half-percent" society. What he meant was that the percentage of Egyptians who determined Egyptian political, economic, and social life, whose decisions held sway, who owned most of the agricultural land, and who enjoyed privileged positions, was no greater than half a percent, while the remainder of Egyptians were completely marginalized. This depiction was largely true. It is also true that a few years after the revolution it was no longer possible to describe Egyptian society in this way. But even after the reversals in economic and social policies following the death of Nasser, it is still impossible to describe Egyptian society today in terms similar to those used by Nasser to describe pre-1952 society. What exactly has happened?

The 1952 revolution undoubtedly contributed to the explosion of the phenomenon of a mass society in a way that was unprecedented in Egyptian history. Its impact can be likened to the sudden rupture of a huge dam that had held back a massive flood. The buildup of pressure behind the dam was partly the result of rapid population growth, and partly due to the spread of education over the previous decades and the concomitant rise in the aspirations of large sections of the population. But the force of this tide was given added impetus by the various laws and measures taken by the revolutionary government, which redistributed income and wealth, and spread education at a rate faster than ever before and increased the rates of industrialization and economic growth. The result was that a rapid growth in population was transformed into the much more significant phenomenon of an increase in the "effective size" of the population, that is, the increase in the number of people with the power to influence the economic, political, and social life of the country through the rise in their purchasing power, and by virtue of their skills and education, and their greater access to the media. This led to repercussions in many aspects of Egypt's social life, as will be shown in the following chapters, but let us refer briefly here to two examples, one related to intellectual life in general, and the other to religious discourse.

There is no doubt that the social mobility witnessed by Egypt during the last fifty years has had an enormous influence on the content of Egyptian literature, and even the social strata to which the writers themselves belong. The same may be said of radio and television programs and the social identities of their presenters, as well as of films and newspapers, and even the language employed by these various media of cultural expression. The rise in the rate of social mobility has been a largely influential factor in this respect, but so too has the absolute increase in the number of people seeking out these cultural commodities. Culture in an era in which the literacy rate is no greater than 20 percent, as was the case in Egypt prior to 1950, cannot be the same as culture in an era in which that rate has surpassed 50 percent, as is the case today. The books and magazines whose readership does not exceed one or two thousand people must contain different things from those publications that are bought and read by tens of thousands. It would be impossible for the culture broadcast to the select few owners of early radio sets to be the same as that broadcast to the near-universal television audience of today. The films and plays that are only viewed by a small middle class must be different from those whose projected audience numbers in the millions and encompasses many different classes.

Let us also look at the changes that have come upon the content and style of religious discourse in Egypt. In my book *Whatever Happened to the Egyptians?* (Cairo: The American University in Cairo Press, 2000), I discussed the changes in religious discourse that arose from the increase in the rate of social mobility. I concentrated particularly on the frustration felt by wide sections of society when their members witnessed the upward progression of many individuals who had until very recently shared the same social class, while they themselves had, for reasons of their own, failed to do the same. I associated that frustration with certain forms of religious extremism and violence, and indicated how ambitious individuals also often used religion as a cover for their ill-gotten gains in status, again a result of rapid social mobility. Now I want to turn to the effect that the increase in population size has had on the form and content of religious discourse.

A religious treatise addressed by an intellectual or a writer, like Sayed Qutb,[2] to a few thousand mostly educated readers, in a book or article that, by its very nature, requires a relatively long period for composition and publishing, must be very different in form and content to a weekly sermon addressed by a television preacher like Sheikh Metwalli al-Sha'rawi[3] to an audience of millions. Readers can appreciate that important disparities must arise by virtue of the sheer differences in number between the two possible audiences be they in the style of discourse,

27

the subject matter addressed, the meanings derived, or the extent to which language style is accorded more importance than content as a means of attracting an audience.

No matter how powerful the currents rippling through society, Egypt was not living in a vacuum, but in the midst of a world that was for its part also passing through profound changes that were bound to affect Egyptian society. I suggested in the previous chapter that one of the most important of the changes that occurred at the end of the Second World War was the rise of the American Era. This era entered Egypt through the gateway of the July Revolution, just as it was the revolution which ushered in the age of the masses.

Most readers would probably agree that had the United States been unwilling to allow the Egyptian armed forces to mount a political movement in 1952, that that movement would not have succeeded. Indeed, it is almost certain that the reason that the British forces stationed along the Suez Canal at that time did not interfere to quash the military coup was a result of American intervention. We also know that the first thing King Farouk did, when officers surprised him at his palace on July 26 with a document of abdication, was to call the American ambassador on the telephone to find out if he agreed with the course of events; when he learned that indeed he did, the king signed the abdication. But apart from all this, could it really have been mere chance, for example, that the revolution took the form of a military coup, as have so many others before

28

and since—the preferred American method of effecting political change in Third World countries after the end of the Second World War? Was it a little too coincidental that the first economic and social reforms issued by the revolutionary government were the agricultural reform laws, the favored American method at the time for containing the spread of communism in various countries?

Or let us review the economic policies adopted by the revolutionary government. The new regime started by accepting the American Four Point Program, which was the first form of U.S. foreign aid after the war. The government came to rely heavily on American food aid between 1958 and 1965, before it was completely stopped by an American decision in 1967. Was this dependence on American aid really necessary to achieve rapid economic development in Egypt, and in the best long-term interests of the country? Many people, myself included, think not, but such food aid was certainly a very convenient method, from the American point of view, of disposing of American surplus food crops in such a way as to help achieve the aims of American foreign policy at the same time. Seen from the angle of purely Egyptian interests, it would seem that it would have been very possible for Egypt, without too great a sacrifice, to have achieved rapid economic development without such a heavy reliance on American wheat and other agricultural products. This would have been much easier to achieve in the 1960s than it was in the 1970s or the 1980s, after Egypt had become addicted to the aid, and it certainly would have been much easier than it is now.

Indeed, the very concept of development that was adopted by the revolutionary government had certain features that proved highly suitable to the fulfillment of American aims in the Third World during the postwar years. The new Egyptian regime adopted the same development philosophy that prevailed worldwide throughout the 1950s and 1960s, was propagated by the various agencies of the United Nations Organization, and which became widely accepted at the time by academics as well as Third World governments without due reflection. We discovered only much later that this view of development was neither the only one possible nor the one most adequate for our purposes. For instance, we accepted a model of development based mainly on increasing per capita income, rather than on the satisfaction of basic needs, which could have meant less economic waste, greater social justice, as well as faster political progress. Instead, the adoption of that philosophy of development allowed the application of economic policies that pandered to the middle class, and encouraged the kind of growth in luxury-good consumption that was unjustifiable in the context of the standard of living of most Egyptians at the time, since the most basic needs of the poorest sections of the population had simply not been met.

Much progress was indeed achieved during the 1950s and 1960s in raising the levels of nutrition, in housing, and in the education of lower income groups, compared with what went on before the revolution, but much more could certainly have been achieved in many areas, most obviously in the eradication of illiteracy. The same bad decisions led to excessive expenditure on armaments and the over-use of capital-intensive methods of production, and may even have been partly responsible for the erosion of political democracy. The two major weaknesses of the development policies adopted were the excessive dependence on American aid and the unjustifiable tendency to accommodate the disproportionate consumerism of the middle class. These two defects, which began on a moderate scale during the 1960s, became much graver in the 1970s and have continued to grow ever more serious since, with many distressing repercussions on Egypt's economic and political life.

In the following chapters I try to show the impact, on several aspects of social life in Egypt over the last fifty years, of the combination of these two phenomena: the rapid growth, both of the "effective size" of the population, and of American influence. Although the net effect has been lamentable in many ways, it has not been a total loss, and there seems to have been something inevitable about the events that took place. Indeed, much of what happened in Egypt during that period could be discerned in other countries as well.

# 3

## Journalism

There is no natural or human law dictating that we must read a newspaper every morning. This rather strange practice grew by stages out of specific economic and social circumstances until it had established itself among large segments of the population. In so-called advanced societies, the habit is so widespread that it has become something of an addiction.

How can it have caught us unawares?

There is, without a doubt, a need to know some news, and this need must be met by one means or another. For example, should a hostile tribe be intent on raiding and plundering a neighboring village, there must be a way for the authorities to warn the inhabitants of the village to take precautions and protect themselves against a possible imminent attack. The best method might be by way of imams in mosques or pastors of churches, the callers to prayer, who might broadcast the announcement from the highest minaret; or someone with a powerful enough voice to raise the alarm in the main square. Any central power undertakes such steps to make important news announcements, such as the general mobilization of troops for war, an increase in the tax levy on a crop, and so on.

These historical antecedents of journalism were perfectly reasonable methods for pre-literate communities. When, in time, newspapers appeared for sale, they did so after the realization of two essential conditions: the advent of printing, and the appearance of sufficient numbers of literate people willing and able to pay the price of a newspaper, which in turn justified the costs of printing and distribution.

The first condition was met in the middle of the fifteenth century with the invention of the printing press, while the second was not met until the beginning of the seventeenth century in some European countries, when the conditions became ripe for the appearance of the first regularly produced newssheets. In the Americas, no regular newssheet appeared until the end of that century (1690), when one appeared in Boston with the ungainly title of "Publick Occurences Both Foreign and Domestick," describing itself as "furnished once a month (or if any glut of occurences happen oftner)." This first American newspaper was small in size, 15cm by 23cm, and no more than four pages long, with three pages filled with short news stories, and the last page left blank for the readers' personal use. In any event, the paper only issued one edition, as four days after its appearance the governor ordered its closure. Daily newspapers arrived about one hundred years later.

The establishment of regular newspaper editions was closely tied to the rise of the middle class, that is, it was a purely bourgeois phenomenon. Most of the first newspapers were concerned with trade news, such as the arrival of a ship in port and a list of its contents. Soon enough, they began adding political news and commentary. However newspapers continued to address the middle class from their first appearance at the beginning of the seventeenth century until the beginning of the twentieth century. They published matters of concern to that class and responded to its tastes, similarly refraining from subject matter that would offend its moral and aesthetic sensibilities. Thus we find that *The Times* of London, which first appeared under the name *The Universal Register,* published a promise from its founders to its readers in its first edition of January 1, 1785, to the effect that the newspaper would contain nothing to wound anyone's sentiments or offend their moral sensibilities. Similarly, when the first editor of the *New York Times* took up office in 1896, he saw it best to adopt the motto "All the news fit to print," and promised that the paper would not "soil the breakfast cloth."

One should not be surprised then to find in these papers articles from the greatest writers of the day, or stories and novels in serial form from the pens of the greatest novelists. So the first British dailies, which appeared in the first half of the eighteenth century, published the serialized stories of Daniel Defoe, author of *Robinson Crusoe*, while the writer of the feature articles in one of them was Jonathan Swift, of *Gulliver's Travels* fame. This was just the start of the participation of many great literary figures and political writers in newspaper writing, from Samuel Johnson, Charles Dickens, and William Thackeray in England, to Goethe and Schiller in Germany, and to Mark Twain in America.

By 1900, the literacy rate and purchasing power of consumers had increased to the point that allowed a newspaper like the British *Daily Mail* to print and distribute one million copies a day. This must have given rise to the bright idea that harnessing this broad demand for newspapers could be profitable to those who could address this wide audience in a way that it liked.

It was soon discovered that more people tend to buy newspapers with provocative headlines in bold type, and with plenty of pictures. If the subject is scientific, the public likes articles to be as simplified as possible; if the subject is politics, then articles should be fiery and exciting. News is best when it is tied to exposing secrets and scandals, and the best stories are love stories, particularly those involving sex.

Among the first newspapers to discover this were the two New York papers *The Journal* and *The World*. Toward the end of the nineteenth century these two papers entered into a fierce competition to attract readers. When one paper published a serialized story entitled "The Yellow Kid," to great public acclaim, the other immediately imitated it. This new fad quickly spread out of New York and across the country, finally reaching beyond the United States. Since then, because of the title of the first story of its kind, this sensationalist style has been known as "yellow journalism." A vicious circle was bound to develop: the increase in readers, arising from an increase in population and purchasing power, led to an increase in demand for newspapers. This increased the temptation for newspaper publishers to cater to the demands of the largest segment of the readership with simple, short, and exciting stories; hence the growth in the yellow journalistic content of the papers. This led to a new increase in readership, and so on. By the middle of the twentieth century, the daily circulation of the *Daily Mail* in Britain had doubled to two million, while the *Daily Mirror* was selling 3.7 million and the *Daily Express* four million copies per day.

When the readership reached these levels, it was only natural that the following step be taken: instead of the newspapers selling their news and features to their readers, they began to sell the readers themselves to advertisers, for when a newspaper's circulation reaches a certain level, it can begin to rely on profits gained from its readership not as readers *per se*, but as purchasers of many other goods. From this point on, it can begin to offer a more costly and profitable service than the more informative and instructive one it had originally provided. This new service is advertising.

With this development, an important transformation in newspaper content was bound to take place. Of course, it was necessary to keep readers interested and entertained, but as the importance of advertisements increased, the importance of credible news or good quality writing had to decrease. Indeed, readers' opinions of the newspaper are probably no longer considered as important as they once were, just as long as they buy the newspaper in the first place. The important thing is that they are persuaded that there is something in the paper worth reading, even if they discover after a short while that what they thought was important turned out not to be so. In that short while, many advertisements are sure to have caught their eye and entered their conscious or unconscious minds.

In journalism, as in many other areas of cultural and social life, we find that a development that took three centuries to happen in Europe has taken a century or less in Egypt. True, the appearance of the first newspaper in Egypt goes back as much as two centuries, when Napoleon started two newspapers upon his arrival in Egypt in 1798, but these were in French for the French. Muhammad 'Ali's newspaper, *Egyptian Events*, was first issued in 1828 in Arabic and Turkish, but it was an official newspaper comprising laws and administrative decrees, without any news that we would recognize as such now. In any case, the publication of a regular newspaper to be read by people all over Egypt was not possible until the postal service was founded in 1875, and until the number of literate people became large enough to justify such a publication.

The literacy rate in Egypt remained below 20 percent until the middle of the twentieth century; until that time, no newspaper existed except for a few read by a very small percentage of the population belonging to the middle and upper classes. The members of those two classes were generally well educated but their number was too small to permit the newspapers to make any income to speak of from advertising. These circumstances determined the type of newspapers and magazines that Egypt would have until the middle of the century: there were extremely limited numbers of copies, and both the language and content had to be suitable to readers of refined tastes; they were non-sensational and included very few pictures. The magazines regularly featured the writings of the most talented writers in Egypt, from 'Abbas al-'Aqqad to Taha Hussein, and from Tawfik al-Hakim to Salama Musa.[4]

The change for the worse came at the end of the Second World War with the appearance of the *Akhbar al-Yawm* school of Egyptian journalism. That was when readers of Egyptian newspapers got their first taste of provocative banner headlines, with scant attention paid to the content of the articles running beneath them. The number of pictures increased, and like the news stories they were chosen for the provocative nature of their content. Some of the great Egyptian writers, such as 'Abbas al-'Aqqad, Tawfik al-Hakim, and Salama Musa, continued writing for the

newspapers and magazines of the *Akhbar al-Yawm* establishment, but the amount of space devoted to such writing
shrank considerably in comparison to the size of the paper.
The owners' excuse for this was that it was not exactly
what the public wanted.

With the revolution of 1952, a new kind of sensationalism
came to newspaper publishing, with heady political subjects being added to the usual exhilarating mix of crimes,
scandals, and the private lives of film stars. The inevitable
result of this was yet another lowering of the standards of
journalistic language and content. This reflected the
demands of more recent readers, who were drawn from
the new members of the middle class, and who had
benefited from the revolution's measures of redistribution.
These new members of the middle class had received an
education of lower quality, in overcrowded schools and
universities, and from teachers who had been churned out
quickly in response to the needs of the rapidly expanding
number of schools.

All this inevitably led to a large rise in the circulation
of newspapers. This rise in circulation could have pro-
pelled advertising as a source of revenue into a prominent position, were it not that during the 1950s and
1960s many newspapers became reliant upon direct government funding. The government had itself founded
several newspapers and wrested ownership from the
founders of others. In addition, the nationalization of
many trade and manufacturing enterprises that took

place at the beginning of the 1960s and effectively granted a monopoly to the state, made it hardly necessary for those companies to advertise.

Despite the accomplishments of the first twenty post-revolutionary years by way of income redistribution and increase in Egypt, the expansion in the relative size of the middle class between 1952 and 1970 cannot be compared to what happened to that same class in the following twenty years, from 1970 through 1990. For all of Nasser's measures of agricultural reform and nationalization, and the provision of a universal free education, these could not match the impact which mass migration to the oil-producing countries of the Gulf had on increasing the size of the Egyptian middle class. Even with the income redistribution policies of Nasser reversed, the decades of the 1970s and 1980s were unable to meet the rising tide of demand for schools and universities, regardless of quality, resulting from the ascent of large numbers of people into the middle class. These members of the middle class, with their new type of education, tastes, and aspirations, defined Egypt's mass culture during the last quarter of the twentieth century, and with it the nature of the newspapers available on the market.

At the beginning of the 1970s, Yusuf Idris, Louis Awad, and Naguib Mahfouz[5] were still writing for the papers, but by the end of the century, they had virtually disappeared, with no writer of comparable caliber taking their place.

The sensationalist press, which began somewhat diffidently before the middle of the century at the hands of

41

Mustafa and 'Ali Amin,[6] transformed itself from short, scattered news pieces, to nationalistic and political incitements in the 1950s and 1960s, to religious exhortations in the 1970s. It further progressed to the excitement of sports items in the 1980s, and to sexual provocation in the 1990s. The politics and national issues of the 1950s and 1960s were simplified to appeal to a much broader readership, paving the way for the oversimplified religious interpretations of the 1970s. This gave way to the catharsis of sports and sex, also highly simplified, for what could be simpler than rooting for one team against another, or declaring oneself to be a fan of one particular film star rather than another?

This growing tendency to "dumb down" spread so widely as to include even those magazines and newspapers that, in the 1940s and early 1950s, had been among the most sober and dignified of publications. These same magazines found that they could not maintain a reasonable level of circulation unless they published photos like those found in the yellow journals, or lengthier sports sections, and hugely simplistic articles on religion, as others were doing. Eventually a style of magazine formerly unknown in Egypt appeared. Relying on flashy photos and stories of the secret, the astonishing, and the bizarre, these lurid scandal sheets proved extremely successful.

Thus has Egypt in no more than one hundred years managed to make great strides along the same route that took European and American journalism more than three centuries to traverse. Indeed, in less than thirty years Egypt

has managed to catch up with a school of journalism that
began one hundred years ago in America with the story of
"The Yellow Kid."

# 4

## Television

It is quite possible that when future historians write the history of the twentieth century, the most appropriate name they might coin for the latter half of it will be "the age of the television," in the same way that the first half of the century might be termed the age of the radio and cinema. Yet neither radio nor cinema has spread around the world in quite the same way or engaged people as much as television has.

Egypt has known the medium for scarcely more than forty years. Even in Europe and America, television did not achieve its amazing diffusion to all levels of society before the middle of the century. In England, when Winston Churchill would stir the resolve of his people for war against the Germans, he relied upon the radio to broadcast his fiery speeches. At that time, America was invading the world not with television programs, but with films from Hollywood. Nevertheless, when the time did come for people to try out the television, they abandoned friends and family to sit in front of it. They reserved the best position in the house for it, accorded it all manner of care and attention, and mounted it on wheels to make it easier to move around. People's love for the television has grown so much that it has become difficult for wives to dislodge their husbands from in front of their television sets, while many American school children spend more time watching television than they do at school.

It is not difficult to shed light on this tremendous success and devoted affection. True, when the radio appeared, there was a magic to it that engendered widespread popularity, but this magic and popularity did not last for long once people had discovered the television. Could this be because seeing exerts a more dominant influence on the psyche than hearing, and television engages both senses? It may be, as one Arab poet said, that "the ear sometimes falls in love before the eye," but that particular poet happened to be blind, and in any case, he was not talking about the general rule but an exception to it. It would seem that people can more easily ignore sounds entering their ears than they can images passing before their eyes. When seated with your family in the same room, is it not impossible to ignore the television, no matter how important the conversation?

It would not be going too far to say that the eye is less

46

discriminating than the ear. If we make an exception for music, which appeals to the emotions far more than it does to the rational mind, we find that oral communication engages the rational centers of the mind much more than visual communication does. It seems that humans respond to what they hear mainly through its content and logic, whereas they are influenced by things that they see in ways only weakly linked to logic and reason. True, a suckling baby is initially more affected by its mother's voice than by the sight of her, but as soon as it opens its eyes onto the world, its sense of sight overtakes its sense of hearing. One could maintain therefore that the eye is more "democratic" than the ear insofar as people probably do not disagree as much about what they see as they do over what they hear.

I still remember how attractive photography was to me when I first discovered it as a small child, and how Egyptian country folk, to whom it was all still new, used to clamor to line up in front of the camera, even the elders among them, in the hope of seeing their own pictures. They did all this just for the privilege of seeing still photos, so it is easy to imagine their reaction to moving pictures, let alone to a medium that synchronizes moving pictures with sound.

Such was the success of the cinema at the beginning of the twentieth century. Even the silent films of the first few decades of the century had an irresistible appeal that made Charlie Chaplin and Laurel and Hardy household names throughout the world. But the cinema was dealt a shattering blow by the appearance of television. The difference between the two was like that between a bus and a private car. The owners of television sets were liberated in the same way that private car owners were liberated from public transport. They could determine their own stops along the route and indeed the route itself; all it took was the turn of a key or the push of a button, and everything started working.

It was not hard for television producers to guess what the returns to them from this astonishing invention might be, and indeed they earned what they had dreamed of and more. In the beginning, television remained, even in the land of its invention, beyond the means of most people. At the same time, there was some resistance to it from some of the upper echelons of society, who saw in it the nearest thing to the tastes of the middle class, and a device that would turn them away from reading books and attending plays. For these reasons, until the end of the 1950s, the television remained confined to the middle class and about 20 or 30 percent of the low-income brackets of the population. While a good proportion of the upper classes refused even to look at it, that did not remain the case for long. By the 1970s, the television had become an essential piece of the furniture in any American or European home.

This short phase of the television's life, in which it was reaching about 40 or 50 percent of the population, part of the middle income strata, was very different from what we see today. The audience at that time was much more sophisticated and educated than it is today. For that reason the programs had to be of a much higher intellectual standard. Anyone who remembers the kind of programs that American and British television had on offer in the 1950s, and compares them with the television fare of today, must be amazed at the difference.

The programs of fifty years ago were less provocative, and relied less on sex and violence and more on persuasion and inspiration for their appeal. In fact they addressed the ear more than they did the eye. With their aristocratic mien, they were closer in spirit to radio broadcasts, and more modest and dignified than film. I still remember, for example, a British weekly program I used to watch while still a student in England in the late 1950s, called "The Brains Trust," in which four or five of the greatest thinkers in England would sit in conversation, with an announcer, no less intelligent or dignified than they, who would direct questions to them from the viewers on subjects as varied as philosophy, history, literature, and so on. There is nothing comparable on British television today. The reason for the change is not that the number of people interested in high culture has declined, but rather that such programs can no longer compete with the huge audiences demanding images in favor of content, and programs that stir the emotions rather than stimulate thought.

The principal reason for this transformation is very simple, trivial even—the reduction in the cost of producing television sets to the point where they have become readily obtainable by the masses. This simple fact, brought about by modest technological advances, has turned cultural and intellectual life on its head. With the increase in the number of viewers came a natural change in their demographic profile, making a change in the programs on offer inevitable to render them more suitable to the tastes of the new majority. Most unfortunate of all, however, has been the effect of the sheer rise in the number of viewers, regardless of their intellectual level or tastes. For this increase created the opportunity for enormous profits, not just for television set manufacturers and broadcasters, but for the manufacturers of every conceivable kind of consumer good, and particularly for the promoters of those goods—better known as advertising companies.

Television advertising did not have much importance throughout the 1950s, except in rich industrial countries, and most of the airwaves remained completely free of it until the end of the decade. From then on, advertising crept into broadcasting little by little until it became the major source of revenue for television stations. As a consequence, advertisements ceased to be aired at a time that was suitable to the programs, and the program subject matter became tailored more and more to the wishes of the advertisers and the manufacturers of goods. This alarming development has disturbing parallels with the relationship between arms manufacturers and the realm of war. Instead of waiting for a war to break out and then raking in the profits from the sale of weapons, the producers and suppliers of arms and munitions may now anticipate and indeed encourage the outbreak of war, in order to stimulate weapons expenditure.

\* \* \*

Television's development in Egypt, and in much of the Third World, followed many of the steps that it had in wealthier nations, but in quicker succession. This is only one of the many examples of change that took decades in technologically advanced societies but just a few years with us. Nevertheless, the steps were basically the same: at first, sophisticated programs addressed a small audience, then standards were lowered to reach a wider audience, and commercials began to appear in between programs, until finally we find ourselves with program content actually being defined by advertising.

Thus, when television came to Egypt at the start of the 1960s, the audience was naturally limited to the small segment of society that could afford the price of a set. At that time, the price was high enough to keep television out of the reach of most Egyptians, who were in any case living in houses without electricity. It was only natural, then, that at the beginning of the decade Egyptian television programs were more sedate and sophisticated in terms of subject matter, the use of language, and seriousness of intent than those we see now. The audience of those days would never have accepted the diminished standards we now see, and its size was not large enough to induce advertisers and producers to exploit the new medium.

With the advent of television to Egypt came a new use of the medium, previously unknown in the more affluent countries but employed widely in most countries of the Third World. This was the use of television by the ruling elite to promote itself, consolidate its hold on power, and attack its enemies. It was employed in many African and some Arab countries, with the aim of legitimizing the concept of a national state and mobilizing diverse tribes toward a single set of goals. Yet even this political use was much more sedate in its early years than it later became, when the television audience grew much larger.

By the beginning of the 1980s, twenty years after television came to Egypt, the whole situation had been turned on its head. The mass migration of labor to the Gulf had increased the buying power of wide segments of society, whose previous circumstances had prevented them from acquiring television sets. Now they returned from the Gulf having amassed small fortunes and bringing with them all kinds of new appliances, foremost of which were electric fans and television sets.

It was inevitable that new programs would appear catering to the tastes of the returnees, and this must have whetted the appetites of goods manufacturers and advertisers for a widening of their markets through television. Advertising techniques were modest at first, with commercial announcements appearing only between programs. Little by little, advertising methods grew bolder as advertisements began to interrupt serials or sports broadcasts as well, and more brazen still, advertisements would sometimes appear immediately after the call to prayer or a musical representation of the same. What is more, during the holy month of Ramadan, hapless viewers found themselves bombarded at all hours by a bewildering and seemingly contradictory mix of advertisements, religious slogans, and spiritual programs.

Television entered a new age with the advent of satellite channels. Suddenly television is able to reach far-flung corners of the globe with a single program in real time. In the blink of an eye, it has vastly increased the size of the audience that can view the same serial, sporting event, or newscast, and, for that matter, the same commercial.

At first this would appear to be a simple development of capacity, that is, a matter of increasing audience size. Nevertheless, the ramifications are much more subtle than that. An increase in the audience demanding goods must lead, as we have seen, to a change in the nature of the goods themselves. Finding themselves able to market their goods worldwide, producers now find that the highest profits can be realized if they succeed in appealing to the tastes and inclinations of a worldwide audience. The goods must, as far as possible, not be confined to local tastes, appealing mainly to French consumers, say, but seeming strange to a Chinese or Korean. It is safest, then, to concentrate on elements with a universal human appeal; better yet, they must appeal to the animal nature of humans. Thus, the safest guarantor of profit is the appeal to the basic shared nature of the French, Chinese, and Koreans, whether they are Christian, Muslim, or Buddhist, white, yellow, black, or brown. Not only should the goods (and their advertising) appeal to as broad a market as possible, so too should the programs and news that carry those advertisements. Scandals may attract the attention of a wide public, yet not all scandals are created equal. Since the aim is to market programs worldwide, it is better to concentrate on things considered equally scandalous by Indians, Arabs, and Americans.

A pretty face can always sell news, all the better if her brand of prettiness appeals to a wide cross-section of tastes. Poor Princess Diana had a face such as this, to her great misfortune, and the paparazzi seized upon her as though she were a gift from heaven. Sports stars, too, have great marketing potential, but it helps enormously if the star is friendly and outgoing—even better if he has an attractive wife or fiancée whom he loves and who loves him, who can be photographed from time to time during a game so the audience can see her reaction when he wins or loses.

The age of globalization brought all this to Egyptian television, and the Egyptian viewers reaped some benefits but also paid a heavy price. With the rapid spread of the satellite dish, millions of Egyptians gained access to images of what was happening in the remotest corners of the earth. Official propaganda began to lose much of its efficacy for there was now a continuous flow of information that was at times directly opposed to it. With the growth of competition from other sources of information and exposure to more independent programs and news analysis, the Egyptian publicly-run television stations had to give way to new privately-run channels that were allowed a greater measure of freedom but were susceptible, nevertheless, to some "friendly" gestures from the government to prevent things from getting out of hand. But competition from foreign television stations was not all for the better, since the prize ultimately goes not to the station that tells the most truthful stories but to the one that can capture the largest number of viewers. These may demand more sexually permissive films and a greater dose of entertainment, but it may also require, particularly if a large and lucrative market exists for it in the rich Arab Gulf states, programs of a more religious and moralistic nature. As a result, Egyptian television has moved, during the last two decades, in these two contradictory directions.

# 5

## The Telephone

It is said that a friend of the famous French painter Auguste Renoir once told him of an astounding new invention that the painter had not yet heard of: the telephone. The friend described how two people could talk to one another even though they were miles apart. Renoir asked: "Suppose the telephone rang while I was absorbed in a painting; should I leave what I am doing to answer it?" His friend answered, "Yes." To which Renoir replied, "How then would I be any different from a servant who comes at my bidding when I ring the bell?"

This grave situation which Renoir predicted and refused to submit to has come true. We have submitted to it completely. We will allow any man, woman, or child to summon us with the telephone bell from any place, and at any time of day or night, no matter what work we may be engaged in, important or not, to answer some obscure or unfathomable interruption, or in anticipation that this particular phone call from some unknown person will fulfill some old hope that has remained unanswered until now.

Could it be that the Wahhabi sheikhs[7] of old were not completely wrong to object to the introduction of the telephone into Saudi Arabia when King 'Abd al-'Aziz first showed it to them about seventy years ago? Like Renoir they were afraid of the harm that the implement might do, but they expressed their fear in rather a different way "Something that can transfer a voice across such wide distances must be a work of the Devil, and for that reason, it must be prohibited under Islamic law." After a while, they ceased their opposition, having succumbed to the view that the matter of prohibition or permission does not lie in the instrument itself but rather in the use to which it is put. This, I suppose, could be said of any new technology, be it the telephone, video, or cinema. Nor indeed, is it very different from the view of the Canadian theorist Marshall McLuhan expressed in his book *The Medium is the Massage* (New York: Bantam, 1967) and aptly summarized in the title of the book. Technology is not a neutral tool: by its very nature it defines the content of the messages transmitted through it, and the nature of the telephone surely exerts a direct influence over what people say to each other and how they say it. But it is also true that the medium itself must change with the development of the society using it. This is what I will try to show in this chapter by tracing the history of the telephone in Egypt over the last fifty years.

I don't recall that the telephone played much of a role in our family life in the 1940s. The bell hardly ever rang, and when it did, the calls were without exception for my father. Moreover, I recall that he would receive calls but that he hardly ever made them. There was little doubt that the telephone was in our house for him and him alone. The calls were always quick, short, and of clear purpose. Nor would it have entered the mind of some foolish boy or girl of the household to use it. Not even my mother could have imagined that she might want to use it, except perhaps to call my married sister, who in any case did not even own a telephone herself.

My first memory involving the telephone centers on the following strange story. It was around 1945, while I was a student in my first years of primary school. In our reading book was a story about a telephone, which the authors must have considered an appropriate subject for modern, sophisticated students to read about. In one of the chapters a boy named Ibrahim asked his friend Khalil, "What is your telephone number, Khalil?" To which Khalil answered, "My telephone number is 62047." That was the number exactly. I still remember it to this day, because that was our own number at home!

How on earth did our telephone number get into our school reading book? It was most likely my own father who put it there, since he was one of the editors of the book. The story needed a telephone number, and he saw nothing wrong with using his own; it never crossed his mind what might happen as a result. What did happen was that every year in about the middle of February, when students got to that chapter of the book, our telephone would begin to ring from about the time students got home from school until the time came for them to go to bed. All of them asked for Khalil. This would continue until the students moved on to the next chapter of the book.

That would take up all of a week or two out of the year. Otherwise the telephone hardly ever rang, and it certainly did not bring anything worth remembering into our life, and we scarcely ever mentioned it. I never remember my father telling one of the children that someone or other wanted one of them on the telephone. If one of my siblings (one of the boys, of course, never a girl) wanted to call someone on the telephone, he would do it while my father was not present, so as not to be thought of as lacking respect. In any case, using the telephone without his permission was physically impossible; it remained fixed in place like a rock and heavy as a cannon on its special shelf on the wall, with its cord too short to allow it to be moved should anyone have ever considered doing so.

No wonder that telephone calls were short and to the point. Only rarely was friendship or anger expressed, much less love or any other human emotion. This was not for any consideration of cost, but for technological as well as social reasons. Technological limitations made it difficult to cart

the telephone around, while the social factor related simply to the number and type of families that owned telephones at that time: I do not think that telephone users in
Egypt in the 1940s could have exceeded 5 percent of the
population. The rural population, which at the time made
up about 80 percent, would not even have known what a
telephone was, except perhaps for the likes of the local
constable and the village headman, and to reach them by
telephone would have been tryingly difficult. City dwellers
viewed the telephone as a luxury that only the social elite
and a few professionals could afford.

Things changed in the 1950s after the revolution opened
the door wide for the growth of the middle class, and the
number of telephones increased quickly, bringing many
other changes along too. The nature of the calls themselves
changed. No longer were they restricted to matters of
pressing importance that could not await a face-to-face
meeting or the arrival of a letter. The telephone would ring
just to convey the season's greetings or a simple "How are
you?". Housewives began to use the telephone to keep up
with their married daughters and sons-in-law; the married
daughters in turn would use it to ask their mothers about
the right way to stuff vegetables; and children used it to
plan trips with their friends or to meet them at the cinema.
One thing remained off limits, which was for boys to call
up their sweethearts, and it was unthinkable for a girl to
call a boy. If a boy were caught making such a call, he
would be severely punished, and if the culprit were a girl,
this would be tantamount to an earthquake, and tongues

would wag about it forever. Fortunately, neither of these things was ever expected or likely to occur.

An important change occurred in the ten-year period between the mid-1950s and the mid-1960s. This was a period of genuine commitment to economic development in Egypt, when Egypt secured fairly large resources from the nationalization of the Suez Canal and foreign aid, in addition to what remained of the sterling reserves it had accumulated during the Second World War. These years saw a great amount of spending on various sectors of the Egyptian economy and were also a period in which great importance was placed on income redistribution to ameliorate the plight of the poor. If it can ever be said of Egypt that it experienced socialism, it was during this period, not before or after it.

All this was reflected in the change that occurred in the use of the telephone. It was only natural that with the great increase in government power and activity, there would be a greater need for the telephone in government departments, not least in those concerned with intelligence and state security. At the same time, the middle class was growing rapidly in response to rapid economic development and income redistribution. So the demand for telephones from private users grew alongside the demands of the government. Yet the government did not regard the expansion of the telephone network as a high priority in its development programs, preference being given to manufacturing and agriculture. Only after delivering telephones to those whose patronage could not be ignored, did the government turn its attention to the demand of others, however pressing their needs may have been.

As a result of this, when I returned to Egypt in the mid-1960s, having finished my studies abroad, and my wife and I set up a home of our own, I found the process of connecting a telephone in my house an exceedingly difficult task. For several years, when I needed to use the telephone I had to leave the house and walk to the corner grocer, who allowed me to use his phone. His charge was small but the real price was his learning many of my family secrets and the details of my work as a university professor. To call relatives in Europe required an even more complicated process, sometimes taking up an entire day, and that was for a call that lasted only three minutes. That was because to make the call, I was obliged to go to the central exchange, pay the price of the call, and tell the operator which number I wanted in Europe. At this point, a grueling set of calls would pass between my operator and the operator at the main telephone exchange in Ramses Street in downtown Cairo. My operator, a good-hearted fellow, generally took pity upon me and would try to talk to his counterpart in flattering tones, calling her "sweetheart" or sometimes "Miss. Radio," until she took pity on both of us and made the call.

It was not much good at that time to hold a title of nobility. Such titles had in any case been abolished in 1953, and the old aristocracy had lost much of its money and all of

its influence. It was much better for you to know an important officer in the military or police, or better yet to know
someone who worked at the Ministry of Communication,
and for that reason the director of the office of the minister of communication was one of the most important of
people in those days, since he had access to the list of
names due to receive home telephones.

These were some of the costs of the socialism of the
1960s. But they were not the only costs nor were they the
most important. The 1960s are associated with a completely new phenomenon: the beginning of the surveillance of
telephone calls for reasons of state security. No one was
able to know whether any particular telephone conversation was actually being monitored or not, but at the same
time, one always felt that one's own telephone might very
well be. Politically active people were subject to intense
surveillance, which was not limited to their telephones. The
mail was monitored as well, since many letters would
arrive after having obviously been opened and resealed,
with a stamp or a sticker affixed stating that it had been
opened by the censor.

Many Egyptians felt that what happened to the telephone
in Egypt during the 1960s was a small price to pay, in light
of the many economic and social advantages reaped by the
lower and middle classes as a result of rapid economic
development and income redistribution. Others did not see
it this way, but what is certain—and agreed upon by all—is
that in the ten years between the mid-1960s and the mid-

1970s (a period that could be described as neither socialist nor capitalist), the burden that we all carried, irrespective of social class, was far too heavy. For in that period, there was no rapid economic development or income redistribution to speak of, and no telephones either.

The 1967 war dealt the Egyptian economy a severe blow to the extent that economic development became exceedingly slow. The army needed rebuilding, the displaced residents of the canal zone had to be relocated, the oilfields of the Sinai peninsula were occupied by the Israelis, the Suez Canal closed, and foreign aid had fallen sharply. The result was not only a great reduction in investment, but also a sharp decline in the maintenance and renovation of aging public utilities, including such things as the vital renovation of Cairo's sewage system.

In such circumstances, what should one expect to happen to the telephone system in Egypt? The demand must of course have continued to grow, but the government did not have the resources to provide for such a luxury. It was not possible to assign to the telephone any priority at all, high or low. By the mid-1970s, the situation had deteriorated to an extent that would have been comical had it not been so tragic. Owning a telephone did not mean very much. There was hardly ever a dial tone. If you lifted the receiver and found one, you were enormously lucky. If you did not, and that happened most of the time, the way you reacted depended on your personality and your mood at the time. It was common for people to give each other advice about the best way to proceed when there was no dial tone. Some advised waiting until the dial tone returned of its own; others thought that waiting was of no avail and that it was more effective to tap on the hook. If the dial tone did return, the chance of your actually reaching the number you had dialed was remote. Here too, people would advise certain ways of dialing, claiming that if you put a certain pressure on the dial, it would get good results. In such a situation, it did not feel so bad for people who had ordered a telephone in the mid-1960s if it had not arrived by the mid-1970s. They began to feel a certain sense of equality with those who had already acquired one, that there was no great difference between having a telephone and not having one.

This state of affairs was by no means confined to the telephone; other utilities were in just as bad a shape. The sewers would overflow every other day or so even in the most prestigious, let alone the less important, neighborhoods of Cairo, and in the smaller cities. Blackouts were common and streetlights often did not work, either because the actual cables or lamps had been stolen or simply because very little was being spent on electricity lines. Water did not reach the upper floors of buildings, and every day some new hole would appear in the old and poorly maintained streets. It was as if someone were punishing Egypt for her bad behavior of the previous ten or twenty years.

With the launching of the open-door policy of the mid-1970s, things began to change, albeit slowly. For the telephone, this manifested itself in a foreign loan of billions of dollars to repair the old network and install new ones, so that by the mid-1980s the telephone situation had changed radically. People stopped talking *about* the telephone and started talking *on* the telephone. For some years after, Egyptians would marvel at the fact that they could hear the dial tone as soon as they lifted the receiver, or the voice of the very person they had dialed to speak to. A tide of people rushed out to buy the telephone, which they referred to at the time as the "instant telephone," prepared to pay the charge for hooking it up however high that might be. Soon that charge became much lower, and the process of connecting a telephone almost an immediate one. Then, with the massive Egyptian emigration to the oil states between 1975 and 1985, large new segments of the population, who had never imagined that they might one day acquire this modern implement, began to purchase telephones. With the improvements to the network and the increase in the number of central exchanges, even the number of telephones in villages began to increase.

By the end of the 1980s, the telephone had ceased to be the aristocratic appliance it had been in the 1940s, nor was it used only by the wealthy middle classes, as it had been in the 1950s and the 1960s. Nor again was it a mute device, like Victorian children, to be "seen but not heard," as it had been during the better part of the 1970s. Instead, it had become an important part of everyday life, to be seen, heard, and used everywhere. Gone was the rock-heavy implement of old, fixed in place by a short cord. It had now been replaced by a lightweight set with a long cord, making it easy to move about, and, a little later, by a cordless telephone.

It is easy to imagine the effect that these advances in technology had both on social relations, and on the content of telephone conversations, for as predicted by Marshall McLuhan, the new medium had to carry a new message. With these profound technological advances, a telephone conversation no longer had to take place within earshot of others, and therefore under the supervision of the head of the household. What is more, with the ease of acquiring a telephone and the increase in the number of people one could call, the monopoly exercised by the head of household over the telephone was weakened. The telephone could be used in any place and for any purpose, important or not. The low cost of acquiring and using a telephone allowed it to spread to most social classes, and since it was no longer used simply for unusual circumstances, the protocols of telephone use underwent a noticeable change. The length of the conversation extended greatly, and that very Egyptian tradition, so different from the European, began to be employed even in telephone conversations, namely that instead of getting right to the point, callers would first have to convey their greetings, and ask about the health of their interlocutors and after their children one after the other. Having done this, the call could not be ended simply after a businesslike exchange of information; instead callers had to back out of the conversation gradually, expressing all sorts of affections and exchanges of best wishes before hanging up. Finally, the Western opening greeting of "Hello" fell out of use to be replaced by the Arabic expression "al-salamu 'alaykum" ("Peace be upon you"), with the increasing numbers of people spending time in the Arab oil states, and the spread of piety among those sections of the population that could afford to have a telephone.

Ten years later a new development arose that few would have expected or dreamed of, for in the late 1990s, Egypt entered the age of the mobile telephone, and the telephone was no longer bound to a particular place by a cord, short or long, nor even to a particular home. Now people could talk on the telephone no matter where they were, at home or on the road, under a roof or out in a field, on the high seas or in the sky. What was strange was that mobile telephones were to be seen on Egyptian streets, in clubs and restaurants, at the universities, and on the beach, more so than in the much wealthier nations of Europe, and that the use of the mobile telephone ran from the richest strata of society all the way down to the lower middle class. But perhaps this should not be that surprising. By now we should have become used to the notion that something invented in the West to fulfill a specific function may be used in a country like Egypt largely as a symbol of social status. After all, the same thing happened with the automobile, the television, the video cassette player, and the satellite dish; it was only natural that it should happen with the mobile telephone.

But there is perhaps something rather more insidious about the mobile phone. Rather than being merely another step in the development of communication technology, its appearance seems to pose a greater threat to human relationships than the old-style, immobile telephone. For now a sudden ring of the telephone, which can be carried anywhere and concealed in the smallest bag or pocket, can interrupt a serious conversation, an intimate discussion, or the most solemn of occasions. There is no doubt that it will ultimately lead to important changes in what people say to each other, confirming, yet again, Marshall McLuhan's view that the medium *is* the massage. But it may go as far as to confirm the Wahhabi sheikhs' worst fears, namely that a device that can carry the voice so far *must* be the work of the Devil.

# 6

## Dress

In my youth, that is, a little more than half a century ago, clothes provided a very easy way to classify Egyptians. Just by looking at someone, you could determine the class to which he or she belonged, whether lower, middle, or upper. This is no longer the case. The abject poor are still easy to distinguish, as are the exceedingly rich, but these two extremes aside, it has become considerably more difficult to identify a person's class by the style of his or her dress.

Fifty years ago it was possible, for example, to classify a person as belonging to the lower classes by two principal articles of clothing. One was the *gallabiya*, which was worn almost without exception by people of this class, whether they were men or women, young or old, or whether they lived in the countryside or in the city. The fabric and color differed between the sexes, but the *gallabiya* was something akin to the official attire of the lower class. It was almost impossible to find a man of that class wearing a shirt and pants, much less a woman—as is so common nowadays. For a man to wear pants in those days made him without question a gentleman, immediately placing him in a different class, but it was difficult to imagine a woman wearing them. The second class markers of fifty years ago were shoes. By this I do not mean the type of shoes worn, but the very act of wearing them. Going barefoot was the predominant trait of the lower class, so much so that the issue of bare feet became one of the greatest themes of social reform during the 1940s.

The *gallabiya* and bare feet were thus the shared features of the men and women of Egypt's lower class at the time, but lower-class women could be distinguished by a third garment: the head kerchief, which has now virtually disappeared. As much as it was common and perfectly acceptable for middle-class women to leave their house without a head covering, the same was considered unseemly for women of the lower class: they were obliged to cover their hair completely for fear of being looked upon with suspicion; for if a house girl showed up at work without her head kerchief, she would be regarded as having descended into the worst type of behavior.

This is now a distant memory. Indeed, most Egyptians are too young even to remember it. Going barefoot has become an exceedingly rare phenomenon in the cities, as even the very poor can afford some sort of shoes or sandals, even if these are made of plastic. Similarly the number of people wearing *gallabiyas* has declined sharply, even among the lower classes, who have exchanged them for shirts and pants, and the lower-class head kerchief has almost disappeared to be replaced by the "*higab*."[8] However, the *higab* has been adopted by women of various segments of the middle class too, so a head covering is, in turn, no longer an easy way of identifying a woman's social class.

My mother used to tell me how very disappointed she had been when she saw my father for the first time, when he came to ask for her hand in marriage. She had been hiding behind the louvers of the window watching for his arrival so as to get a first look at the man who would probably be her husband. She was terribly disappointed to see him wearing the headgear and caftan of a traditionally educated man.[9] What she had been hoping for was someone dressed in a European suit, which she viewed as a sign of modernism and hence a better treatment of women, as well as perhaps a sign of good humor. She married him anyway, and I do not recall her ever having placed any importance on the style of my father's dress after that, nor did she associate his severity and lack of humor with it. As the years went on, she probably discovered that there was no relationship between these two things. This must have become abundantly clear to her when my father, after much hesitation, opted for a

European style of dress, without any discernible improvement to his sense of humor or a relaxation of the strictures
he imposed on my mother and sisters.

Middle class men's dress was of two types: the dress of
the clergy and of the layman, and the Western style. At
mid-century, the former was much more common than it
is now, since an Azhar education had been the most common one through the 1930s, and the numbers of non-
Azharis in schools remained small. Those with an Azhar
education persisted in wearing traditional dress even after
attaining to a not inconsiderable sophistication in modern
culture, and even if their work had no relation to theology.
My father continued to wear the caftan and headgear for
many years until he moved from being a judge of Islamic
law to being a teacher of Arabic literature at an Egyptian
university. There, several of his colleagues who had been
educated in Europe persuaded him that the teaching of
Arabic literature was one thing, and the traditional caftan
and headgear were quite another. Nevertheless, it took him
a long time to stop feeling estranged and bashful in front
of his colleagues and students when wearing European-
style clothes.

When I recall my childhood memories of my father, I do
not find any difference between his dress and that of a man
of his class today, with the exception of three or four
details. First of all, he always wore the red *tarboush*[10] right
up until the day he died in 1954. Soon after that, owing to
the influence of the revolution of 1952, the *tarboush* dis-

appeared completely, as a remnant of Turkish rule, along with aristocratic titles and the old names of military ranks. I remember with amazement how my own generation was obliged to wear the red *tarboush* to school until we passed primary school at the age of eleven or twelve. We also wore short pants. The whole effect—short pants, jacket, and tie, finished off by the red *tarboush* with its characteristic black tassle—must have presented a laughable figure to anyone from a younger generation, but at the time, it all seemed quite natural.

My father also carried a dapper walking stick, upon which he would occasionally lean. Although he did not really need it, it was one of the accessories of the well-dressed man of the day, but it is no longer so regarded. He also carried a beautiful ebony-handled horsehair fly whisk. The whisk's frequent use then and its complete disappearance now indicate several things, one of which is that the level of public hygiene was lower then than it is now, and that technological innovations, such as the refrigerator, air conditioning, and window screens have rendered the fly whisk obsolete. Perhaps just as important is the increasingly fast pace of life; men no longer idle away long hours in coffee houses, trading talk and swatting flies. Furthermore my father did not wear a wristwatch; instead he had a gold pocket-watch with a chain and a fob that tucked into his waistcoat. My parents' generation viewed a watch as something akin to jewelry, the loss of which would be an irremediable disaster.

Only in such minor details did my father's clothes differ

from those of the middle class men of today. This is not the case with women's clothing, which has seen a profound, indeed revolutionary change over the last fifty years, reflecting the rapid transformation of the life of Egyptian women during that period, mainly as a result of their greater participation in public life, particularly in the workplace.

What I remember about women's dress from my childhood is my mother's singular attachment to the color black. I do not recall ever seeing her outside the house wearing anything other than a black dress and headscarf. This was how practically all the women of her generation and class dressed once they had reached adulthood. Anything else would have been seen as something close to exhibitionism. Even the range of colors worn by unmarried girls was restrained and limited, a far cry from the flamboyant colors they wear today.

That was how it was with the dress of the five or ten girls in my class at the school of law at Cairo University at the beginning of the 1950s. There was nothing in the color or design of their clothes to attract attention, and they moved with the utmost modesty among the thousand other male students of the class. Not one of them wore either trousers or a *higab*. Even so, when I look at photos of the students from that era, I am surprised at the styles of clothes worn by the girls, as they invariably appear to be the wrong size and utterly lacking in any sense of style. How can one interpret this? Does it mean that members of the middle class felt more confident in those days than they do now, that simply the kind of clothes they wore was sufficient to distinguish them from the lower classes, irrespective of style? As I have remarked, the lower classes wore highly distinctive, immediately recognizable clothing, but it is also the case that many women still produced much of their daughters' clothing themselves at the time, far more so than they do today. The Singer sewing machine was a permanent fixture in middle class homes, and an essential element of a young girl's trousseau, while the inability to sew was seen as a hindrance to a girl's chances of getting married. The old-fashioned machines, the kind my mother used, were completely hand-operated and required great skill. She would run the machine with one hand and feed a piece of cloth under the needle with the other. Later machines were operated by pedals, and it was one of these fine machines that my sister used after she got married, but with nothing like the frequency with which my mother had used her smaller and less sophisticated machine.

My sister had far less use for her sewing machine than my mother had because of an important development in Egypt's economic life, namely the appearance of ready-made clothing. This came about as a result of the growth of a middle class able to purchase such clothing in sufficient quantities as to lower production costs. The appearance of ready-made clothing led to the disappearance of other customary activities that had been quite common fifty years ago, such as the widespread custom among middle class women to knit woolen garments for their family members. Sewing machines gradually began to disappear from middle class homes, while traditional professions like those of the seamstress and tailor, which had been quite a common feature in the lives of this class, also began to disappear for the same reason. With the less frequent visits of the seamstress to middle class homes, marriageable girls had to discover other ways of finding a suitable husband, because it was mainly the seamstresses who had brought them news of eligible young men as they traveled from home to home.

It is understandable that the habit of buying ready-made clothes did not become widespread in Egypt until the 1960s, for it was only then that the Egyptian middle class became sufficiently large to form a credible market. It was also understandable that items of ready-made clothing began to appear in order of need, beginning with shoes and stockings, then shirts and pants, and only later, jackets and suits, which did not become widespread until the late 1970s.

When my father wanted to purchase some clothes for us he would take us to one of the emporia in downtown Cairo's Fouad Street (now 26 of July) or 'Ataba Square, most of which had foreign names like Avarino, Cicurel, Chemla, or Sednaoui. The garment industry was the preserve of non-Egyptians and Europeans, many of them Jews or Levantines, mainly Lebanese and Palestinians. There were a few exceptions to this rule—small Egyptian-owned stores, the most important of which was the chain of the

Egyptian Manufacturers' Marketing Company, founded by the Misr Bank—but these were tiny islands in a sea dominated by non-Egyptians. And so the situation remained until the end of the 1950s, when the sweeping nationalization of foreign property occurred as well as the wave of Egyptianization that overtook industry and commerce.

I will try to convey some idea of the development of Egyptian clothing from the early 1960s until the present day by describing what I myself have seen over the years in the commuters of the Helwan train line of what is now the Cairo Metro. A ticket from the suburb of Ma'adi to Bab al-Luq in the center of town cost three piasters at the beginning of the 1960s.[11] You could either pay at the ticket window or wait until you boarded, in which case you would pay a surcharge, bringing the cost up to five piasters—if the conductor ever showed up, which was rare. That meant that the ride was effectively free for most passengers. In those days, most passengers wore *gallabiyas*, and the number of women completely covered or wearing the *higab* was negligible. The train would also be full of barefoot children running about among the passengers hawking small items like mint drops, combs, and charms to ward off the evil eye.

When I observe the passengers of the same train line today, I rarely see someone wearing a *gallabiya*, even though this was once the only style of clothing worn by tradesmen. Nor do I see anyone barefoot. The number of women commuting to and from work has increased dramatically, to the extent that they may outnumber the men at certain hours, while most of them now wear the *higab*. However, I have noticed that the variety of styles of the *higab* has increased over the past few years, including the range of colors worn and the manner of its fastening on the head. Beyond that, more and more women now allow a small patch of hair, however small, to show through, and those women who previously took pains with their hair now spend the same effort on their makeup. Indeed, it would appear that wearing the *higab* is no longer inconsistent with wearing stylish clothes, such as a belt to accentuate the waist, a tight skirt, or even pants, an item of clothing which no woman would have even considered wearing forty years ago. [12]

Upper class attire, as seen in magazines and films, was characterized in many cases by an extraordinary permissiveness in terms of which parts of the body, such as the chest or arms, that were left uncovered, let alone the hair. It would never have occurred to female members of the middle or lower classes to be so daring as to leave their hair down. Nor could these two classes have afforded to import all of their clothing from abroad as the rich did, much less sport all the jewelry that glittered from the necks, arms, and ears of ladies of high society. But here again, the differences in appearance between the members of the upper class and of the other two classes were huge and far greater than any differences across classes that we see today. It was unimaginable, for instance, that an Egyptian millionaire of the 1950s (and millionaires were scarce in those days) would wear such a thing as a pair of blue jeans, or that his wife would cover her hair with a *higab*, as may well be the case today. To be sure, disparities in wealth and income are far greater today than they ever were in the 1950s, but equally, expensive clothes are no longer the reliable class indicator they once were. For that purpose, other much more lavish items of expenditure may be in order, such as foreign cars, foreign schooling for one's children, a house at the seaside, or an extravagant wedding or engagement party.

# 7

## Romance

When my heart opened to love for the first time, there was no possible way I might have expressed this love to anyone but to the girl next door. That was over fifty years ago, at the end of the 1940s, and romance in Egypt in those days was an entirely different creature from what it is today.

We were a family dominated by boys. Of eight children, only two were girls, and they were more than fifteen years older than me. For that reason, I have hardly any memory of a female presence in the house except for that of my mother. Neither did any of my sisters' friends ever visit our house. I do not think that it was common in those days anyway. Girls hardly ever ventured out of their own homes, except to attend school for a few years, and then it was off to their husbands' homes. Nor did I have any cousins to whom I could direct my new-found feelings, since I was younger than they and therefore not a suitable candidate for marriage.

In those days all that adolescent girls thought about was marriage. There were no mixed schools in Egypt except for some of the foreign schools, and the only Egyptians who attended those were the children of the upper class. Indeed, sending a girl to school was not seen as a self-evident good, and putting her all the way through secondary school marked a family out as being enlightened and ahead of its time.

Fifty years ago the famous sporting clubs, such as al-Gezira Club in Zamalek, the Heliopolis Club in the neighborhood of the same name, or the Shooting Club in Dokki were sporting clubs in the true sense of the word, not, as they have now become, meeting grounds for boys and girls, or a place to lounge about and talk. Club members would go there with the explicit purpose of practicing sports like tennis, squash, or swimming, and were drawn almost exclusively from the upper classes. Middle and lower class men frequented coffee houses, while women did not go anywhere at all.

In this wretched situation, who could have possibly been the object of my love, apart from my parents of course, except the girl next door? In that, there was no difficulty or lack of opportunity whatsoever. Windows and balconies faced one another, and the summer weather was hot, so that windows were always wide open. It was easy for a girl to throw a smile at the boy next door from behind the backs of her mother and brothers, or to appear on the balcony for some necessity, like hanging out the washing, or to suddenly be overcome with affection for her little brother and shower him with kisses when she knows that the boy next door is watching.

Now the whole thing may seem quite pathetic, since this was the most we could do to satisfy our need for love, but in fact, when you think about it, everything we could have desired was possible in those days, even with the girl next door, with the exception of one thing: touching. All the other intoxicating emotions associated with falling in love followed their usual routine: the exchange of smiles and glances, occasionally even some words, the burning anticipation of the appearance of the beloved after an absence, quarreling and making up, and so on. Even so, all of this eventually led to naught, because the whole thing could end suddenly and without warning when the boy saw his sweetheart through the window getting ready for an engagement party or wedding. Then he would know that another of the neighboring boys, a little older than himself, old enough to dare to ask for her hand in marriage, had indeed requested her hand, and so the whole affair ended as irrationally as it had started.

The situation was no better at university. At law school in a first-year class of no less than a thousand students there were maybe five or six girls. They would sit in the first row of the lecture theater dressed in the most modest of fashion. They did not wear the *higab* or any other head covering, but they did not go to the coiffeur either, a custom that did not start to take hold among Egyptian girls until only twenty or thirty years ago. It was not so easy for those young women themselves. Imagine their position, as they entered the vast lecture hall before a thousand young men all watching them hungrily. No wonder that they would all enter together, clinging to one other uneasily, and leave immediately after the lecture, the time of which was known precisely by their parents, so that the girls could escape to the inviolable sanctuary of their homes.

There was hardly any hope for any of those thousand young men to attract any of these five or six bashful young women. Our hopes, and those of the boys in other colleges, were pinned on the Faculty of Arts. In those days it was famous for being full of beautiful girls. It was the faculty considered at the time to be the most appropriate for girls, being the college of beautiful things like foreign languages, literature, and poetry. There they could wile away their time in the study of the least demanding subjects until the time came for them to make a good marriage. Anyway, there was no harm in their learning some foreign language or reading a bit of world literature as they sat waiting for a husband. As the wives of the future, their children may even benefit from their learning, while the study of law, engineering, or medicine, presupposes a job after graduation, something most parents did not envision for their daughters, and which all husbands would simply refuse to countenance.

When I finished my higher studies abroad in the mid-1960s, and returned to teach economics at 'Ain Shams University, things had changed quite a bit. The proportion of girls among the university students had increased tremendously so that they now made up about a quarter of the total student population. This accorded the girls a boldness they had not previously possessed. Sporting clubs, which had previously been the exclusive preserve of the upper class, had been compelled to open their doors to the middle class, which allowed greater occasion for the mixing of the sexes. There were many more coeducational schools, and not all of them were foreign, nor were all their students from the upper class. But the really surprising phenomenon, which began to appear in Egyptian society around the mid-1970s, and which many saw and still do as a step backward, since, in their view, it implied greater restrictions on women and on relations between the sexes, was the increasing number of women who felt inclined or obliged to cover their hair with the *higab*. In my view, this phenomenon may indeed mean exactly the opposite, as I will now try to explain.

From the beginning of the 1950s, Egypt witnessed numerous developments that, far from increasing restrictions on women, on the contrary awarded them more freedom of movement, increased involvement in public life, and a greater participation in work outside the home. There was, for example, the great expansion of education of both boys and girls, but particularly of girls, as well as the rapid pace of development and industrialization during the 1950s and 1960s, which created greater opportunities for employment of both men and women, and the rapid growth in government jobs that absorbed a great number of university graduates with no distinction between men and women.

All of these factors first appeared in the early to mid-1950s, when agricultural reform led to a decline in domestic work and an increase in the demand for agricultural labor. They persisted through the 1960s, increasing in force until inflation arrived in the 1970s, creating a huge incentive for women to work outside the home in order to augment their husbands' or fathers' incomes. Gradually men began to accept and indeed welcome the idea of marrying a working girl instead of clinging to the old notion that a wife should remain at home after marriage, even if she had been working beforehand. At the same time, the number of people emigrating to find work in the oil-rich states increased, with men being obliged to leave their families at home in Egypt. This placed additional burdens on housewives, who were compelled to perform various functions outside the home that had previously been taken care of by their now absent husbands. The idea of women working and participating in public life became increasingly acceptable, and was encouraged by the media, with Egyptian women gaining a self-confidence they had previously lacked. They gained all this at a small price, namely to cover their hair with the *higab* and to dress more modestly than women with higher incomes were accustomed to doing. Put differently, Egyptian women who had left the protective security of their homes and households, either by free choice or force of circumstance, felt obliged to send a message to the men who shared the same room at a government agency; the same bus, train, or taxi traveling to and from work; or the same bench in a university lecture hall, and so on. This message was sent through the *higab*, and it read: "Yes, I have left the house, but that does not mean that I have become public property. I speak to men and sit next to them, but touching is off limits, as are any attempts to transgress the necessities of the workplace."

All this was completely natural and understandable; but it was also completely natural that it did not prevent a veiled young woman from occasionally falling in love. She may be wearing the *higab*, but her heart is not made of stone. In truth, the likelihood of this occurring was bound to increase with the newly acquired self-confidence of Egyptian girls, their increased contact with members of the opposite sex, and their wider exposure to new cultures and lifestyles. If we find it so strange to see the wonderful sight of young men and their (veiled) sweethearts walking along the Nile, all dressed up in their finery, sometimes holding hands, and exchanging talk and smiles, we should ask ourselves: is this not so much better and more natural than stealing glances at the girl next door from behind the window shades?

I recently found myself in front of the aquarium gardens

in Cairo's Zamalek district. I had an hour to kill before going to an appointment nearby, so I thought I might go in and enjoy the beautiful grounds, which I had not seen for fifty years. I might perhaps relive a few memories of youth, and see whether the years had treated the garden the way they had treated me. The first thing I noticed was that there was now an entrance fee, whereas in my day it had been free. The ticket seller at the window looked tired, weighed down by the cares of this world, but there was nothing unusual about this. What *was* surprising was that he almost tore off two tickets from the book before I even asked for one, then looked taken aback to learn that I only wanted one. I discovered why when I entered the park. The whole place was full of couples dotted about on the benches and pathways, all of them lost in conversation. Some looked slightly embarrassed as a stranger like me passed by, but most were completely absorbed in themselves, each completely delighted with the other. There was not a single unveiled woman among the couples that were there, and yet, at the same time, not one of them appeared stiff or impassive in a desperate attempt to hide the perfectly natural feelings she was experiencing, something I had been used to seeing in young Egyptian women fifty years ago.

# 8

---

# Birthdays

As the youngest member of my family, with five boys and two girls older than myself, I can attest with confidence that not one of my brothers or sisters ever had a birthday party. Because I was the youngest, I was the only one to catch this fashionable new custom that had at the time only recently arrived in Egypt. It quickly spread like wildfire from one social class to another and it might be interesting to examine what it was about Egyptian society that allowed birthday parties to become so popular.

One may well be justified in celebrating the end of the first seven days of a child's life,[13] since mortality rates are high in the first few days of life. For the same reason, it may also be reasonable to celebrate after a year has passed.

But to celebrate the event year after year must have seemed quite silly and entirely unjustified to successive generations of Egyptians.

It was not at all strange that my father never celebrated his own birthday or even called our attention to it. We never paid any attention to it either, and if the truth be known, my father was unsure of the exact date recorded on his birth certificate, for the simple reason that his parents had never applied for a birth certificate, and he had had no need of one until many years later. He seemed sure of the year of his birth but the actual day was a matter of guess-work. Births were not accorded the importance they are now, for both births and deaths were far more common than they are now. A birth certificate was not required for starting school, and it was common for a man to wait until he had started a government job before applying for one. Even then, it was sufficient to get a certificate of age estimation, not an actual record of birth. For women, the need for a certificate was even less. It was rare for girls of my mother's generation, at the beginning of the century, to go to school, and rarer still for them to have a job.

No wonder that my mother did not even know the year of her birth, let alone the exact date. She would laugh when she saw me inviting classmates to my birthday party, and when some brought presents, she would make a show of complaining, "No one ever brings *me* birthday presents!" When we replied in our defense that no one knew when *her* birthday was, she would continue the jest, saying, "It's tomorrow. Everyone should bring me presents then."

My parents saw the whole issue of birthday parties as a childish diversion. They neither thought of throwing a party for me, nor felt that the occasion merited one (I had seven brothers and sisters who had done just fine without one). They did not even make a show of joy on the occasion. I do not recall ever receiving a birthday gift from my parents and, indeed, I ask myself if I ever received a gift from them on any occasion at all.

Birthday parties then were an unfamiliar custom, that had come to us from the West. Even in the West of a hundred years ago, birthday celebrations were nowhere near the familiar custom that they are today. The convention must have been closely associated with the rise of the affluent society, the growth of consumption, and the increasing indulgence shown to children as a result. One need not agree wholeheartedly with the statement I once read describing childhood as a bourgeois invention. Look at how the poor of any country treat their children. All family members are obliged to contribute whatever work they are able to perform in order to ease the burden of life for the whole family. If a girl of seven or eight can do the washing or housecleaning, she does it. If a boy can go out to sell newspapers to augment the family income, he must do it. For such families, the very idea of birthday parties must seem foolish and in quite bad taste.

My own family was not poor; we were of modest means, but my parents continued to uphold the values of a poor society, which had little time for frivolities such as birthday parties for children. Compare then with now: parents know exactly when their precious little darlings' birthdays are coming. When the day arrives, the well-wishing begins in the morning, and the child is showered with gifts from all quarters—parents, uncles, aunts, and friends all use the most careful tactics to ensure that their gifts will be no less expensive or smaller in size than those of the others—and money is spent without limit to make the birthday boy or girl happy. The children in turn examine the hands of the next visitors to greet them before even glancing at their faces, in order to assess the size and kind of gift they will receive. The gift is scrutinized for a moment or two, before the child moves quickly on to the next. In the end, the whole room inevitably becomes piled high with gifts, many of which the child will hardly ever look at again.

This change in attitude to birthday parties during the last fifty years reflects other important changes that have occurred to Egyptian society during that time. First of all is the change in attitude toward children. The prevalent view of children when I was a child myself was the one which had held sway for centuries: children are the natural and inevitable product of marriage, and their function is the preservation of the species. The imperative, then, was to have as many as possible, so that the largest number possible may survive. It is important to protect them and to guard their health, but the true guarantee of their well-being is in the hands of God. A moral upbringing is essential, and education is desirable, but there are strict limits to what two parents can do to form a child's personality, and to mold his or her character, for children are born with their destinies pre-determined. Of course, it was hoped and prayed that children would grow up to be materially successful, and that some of that success would naturally redound to their parents. But using one's children to boast and gain social status, in the manner that we see today, is an entirely different thing. Now children fulfil the same function for their parents as the acquisition of goods. Expensive clothing for children shows off their parent's wealth, as does their enrolment in an expensive private school. All that lavish expenditure necessitates having fewer children, although the birth rate was already falling in response to the lowering of the mortality rate.

The pervasive view of children today is that they are like shapeless lumps of clay that the combination of good parenting and schools can mold in any fashion the parents so wish. This has led to much greater concern on the part of parents for the way they treat their children, and their attitudes have changed from extreme fatalism to an over-confidence in their ability to determine the future and a desire to challenge things that cannot really be changed.

Much of what can be observed in children's birthday parties today reflects this change of attitude to childrearing. Indulging our children with gifts and luxuries reflects partly a belief in our ability to form their personalities. But technological developments also have a part to play. Consider, for example, the number of photographs now taken at birthday parties to record the historic occasion in detail for posterity. The camera did not play much of a role in my childhood, and in any case, pictures could rarely be taken indoors. If a picture was to have any chance of exposure, it had to be taken in direct sunlight with the subject facing the sun. Now anything is possible: pictures can be taken anywhere and in most lighting conditions. And with the advent of movie cameras and video films, birthday parties are recorded for posterity not just by a series of photographs, but by entire talking movies.

With the increase of such "necessary" goods and services required for the birthday celebration and with the increasing numbers of guests, parents began to feel incapable of rising to their duty, worried that their houses were not up to such an elaborate ceremony. So emerged the custom of celebrating birthday parties outside the home: at a club or sometimes even at hotels, and families began to resort to outside help in the form of specialist children's entertainers who could arrive at a party dressed in animal suits, for example, or to perform magic tricks.

If my parents had witnessed any of this, they would no doubt have been stricken with amazement. Perhaps what would have shocked them most would have been the sheer amount of expenditure required for so many ceremonies and rituals. This change in the way people view birthday celebrations was no doubt partly the result of a rise in incomes and of greater contact with the West, but it also relates to the vast increase in the size of the middle class. The lower classes did not and still do not celebrate their children's birthdays; indeed it is doubtful that they even remember birthdays at all. The smaller upper class, because of its much older contact with the West and its high income, always celebrated birthdays, but did so behind closed doors. Now it is the middle class which celebrates birthdays when previously it had not, and it does so for all to see.

# 9

## Culture

A little less than fifty years ago, in 1955, a book written by two young Egyptian Marxists caused widespread reverberations and sparked off great interest among intellectuals in Egypt and throughout the Arab world, who either sang its praises or condemned it vehemently. The attention was well deserved, as the book proved in time to be a milestone in Egypt's intellectual history.

The book was *On Egyptian Culture,* by Abd al-'Azim Anis and Mahmud al-'Alim. The tone of some of its chapters was excessively harsh on some of the great Egyptian writers but the position it expressed was bold and timely, as it reflected the powerful mood of discontent that had been building up among Egyptian intellectuals over the

perceived class bias dominating Egyptian intellectual life
at the time. In essence, the book pointed out that the prevailing intellectual climate completely ignored the needs,
sentiments, and problems of the great majority of the
Egyptian people, the poor and socio-economically
oppressed majority.

This observation was certainly correct, and the time for
promulgating it was ripe. The revolution of July 1952 had
occurred only three years before the book was published,
and one of the proclaimed goals of the revolution had been
to satisfy the basic needs of the majority of Egyptians, to
advance their economic condition, and to put an end to the
glaring manifestations of social injustice. And here were
two eloquent young intellectuals calling for the same thing
in the field of culture.

Years have passed and the Egyptian cultural scene
today bears very little resemblance to that of fifty years
ago. It is almost impossible that those who lived in Egypt
in 1955 and reported on the state of its cultural scene
could have anticipated the kind of problems they might
see today. Old problems have been solved, or have at
least taken on different guises from those of 1955, but
newer and graver complications have risen to the surface
in the meantime, inviting even more severe criticism
than the kind which appeared in *On Egyptian Culture*
half a century ago.

Whatever the case may be, it is certain that the basic
problem today is not the class bias of fifty years ago, but
something else entirely. What, then, could be regarded as

the basic characteristics of the current cultural climate in Egypt? And what are its most visible aspects?

The story had better be told from the beginning, which was well before 1955. It is possible to discern a certain pattern, almost a law, governing the development of Egyptian cultural life throughout the past one hundred years, indeed since the appearance of the first leaders of the Egyptian cultural renaissance in the final quarter of the nineteenth century. This pattern seems to me to be closely connected with the changes that occurred in the characteristics as well as the relative size of the Egyptian middle class.

Let us agree from the outset that among the most important determinants of the cultural climate of a society at any given time are the characteristics of its middle class. This seems to be as true of Egyptian society as it is of any other, and the reasons are not hard to find. It is mainly from members of the middle class that the intellectual products of any society originate, and it is the members of that middle class who constitute the vast majority of consumers of such products. The educational and income levels of the lower class render it unable to play an important role in the production or consumption of culture. As for the upper class, its problem arises not from factors connected with education or income, but from two other factors: its ever smaller size relative to the total population, as well as its lack of a strong enough incentive to excel either in the acquisition (consumption) of culture or in its production, since it has alternative and usually stronger sources of self-assurance. If members of the upper class do participate in either the production or consumption of the culture of which they are a part, it is mostly as dilettantes seeking diversion or amusement. It is left mainly to members of the middle class who are endowed with sufficiently powerful incentives toward advancement and upward mobility, to either catch up with those above them or simply to distinguish themselves from those below. It is the middle class which has traditionally led the way in changing society for the better, and has therefore played the most important role in its advancement. There are exceptions, of course, to be found, in world history as well as in Egypt, of great intellectuals who were members of either the aristocracy or of the lower classes. Such exceptions, however, have always been few in number. It is also true that most European writers, thinkers, and artists (at least prior to the nineteenth century) needed the patronage and support of the aristocracy, whereas the European aristocracy itself rarely produced important writers, thinkers, or artists. This same observation applies to Egypt over the last two centuries.

All this is more or less self-evident. What is also true, however, if not as immediately obvious, is that the middle class does not always display the same attributes and characteristics across time and space. Instead, these vary from one society to another and from one era to the next. We hear a great deal of praise for the middle class in general: for raising the banner of progress, vouchsafing economic development, guarding democracy, and so on. This immoderate admiration and hope is probably the result of a mistaken extrapolation of the European experience to other societies, on the assumption that the characteristics of the European middle class during the first centuries of modern European civilization are necessarily the same as those possessed by the middle class in other societies and in other periods. It would perhaps be more accurate to say that since each middle class acquires and is influenced by the social and economic characteristics of a particular time and place, it can play either a positive or a negative role in the cultural advancement of its nation.

Two of the characteristics of a middle class that perhaps play a decisive role in enhancing or obstructing cultural progress are the nature of its main source of income and wealth, and the speed at which income increases and wealth is amassed. These two characteristics are inter-linked. The speed at which income is increased and wealth is accumulated is one way of expressing the rate of social mobility. A rise from the lower class to the middle class might happen over a long period, taking the better part of a lifetime. This is what usually happens when the source of upward mobility is education, or the growth of industry or trade under relatively stable circumstances. On the other hand, income can increase and wealth be amassed overnight, as a result of capturing an opportunity that aris-es out of runaway inflation, migration to a more wealthy country, or some illegal use of authority. It is natural that a middle class that grows under the former conditions should manifest certain psychological characteristics and moral qualities that are quite different from those of a middle class that has grown and increased in wealth over a much shorter period and by practicing largely unproductive or illegal activities. The impact on the cultural life of the country must also be different in one case from that in the other.

Such differences may be the source of the error in measuring the conditions in the Third World against those in the industrial countries with respect to the characteristics of the middle class and its role in cultural development. The development of a middle class in industrialized nations over the seventeenth to nineteenth centuries was considerably slower than the development of the same class in many Third World countries over the past half century. What is more, the growth of the middle class in the industrialized nations was built upon wealth generated mainly through the development of industry, agriculture, and other "productive" activities, while the growth of the middle classes in many Third World countries relied to a large degree upon rental income, that is, income incommensurate with effort, often resulting from having monopoly power over some economic resource or having some access, often illegal, to authority.

Things were not always this way in Egypt. Rather, over the past one hundred years, the Egyptian middle class has passed through periods in which it manifested varied characteristics. But the Egyptian intellectual climate has also passed through similar variations. In this chapter, I will try to show that the former variations can throw important light on the latter. The period I cover here is much longer than the one we have dealt with so far, since I start as early as the beginning of the British occupation in 1882; however it is only the last fifty years which I shall examine in any detail.

Throughout the three decades falling between the beginning of the English occupation of Egypt and the outbreak of the First World War (1882–1914), the middle class in Egypt remained extremely small compared to what it is now, in both absolute and relative terms. The two main sources of the increase in middle-class income were the growth of agricultural income and the expansion of education. In fact, this class owed its initial formation to individual land concessions from the days of the Khedive Sa'id and to the advancements in education achieved during the reigns of Muhammad 'Ali and Isma'il[14]. Income growth from these two sources was by nature relatively slow, for under normal social conditions, with no runaway inflation, no wars or revolutions, and no sudden opening up to the world economy, the wealth generated by agriculture and education can increase only at a slow rate.

The Egypt of this period witnessed a rarefied cultural climate when compared with preceding eras or with most of those to follow. And this was just as true of intellectuals who clung to tradition as of the modernizers who advocated the adoption of Western ways. This was the period that produced the likes of Muhammad 'Abduh in theology, Qasim Amin and Farah Antun in social commentary and analysis, Muhammad al-Muwilhi and al-Manfaluti in literture, Mahmud Sami al-Barudi in poetry, and Muhammad 'Usman in music. It also saw enormously successful innovations in journalism and the theater. It is astonishing to know, for instance, that Muhammad 'Abduh, an Egyptian son of the soil, who owed his rise in social status to nothing more than an education and native intelligence, exchanged letters with some of the greatest minds of his day, like Tolstoy, and expressed bold, original ideas with the greatest of self-confidence and in elegant Arabic, the likes of which have rarely been seen since.

Such a cultural climate might be explained largely by reference to the two factors adduced above: the main sources of income for the middle class and the relative stability of social conditions for this class. It might also be partly explained by the nature of the relationship of Egypt to the Western culture of the period. The intellectuals of the day had opened up to the West, having either seen it for themselves, or been strongly exposed to it. Nevertheless, they remained rooted in their Arab and Islamic heritage, and even those among them who advocated adopting as much as possible from the West retained a greater confidence and pride in their own culture than did succeeding generations of westernizers. This attitude may once more be partly explained by reference to the same two economic and social factors: the nature of the main sources of income and socio-economic stability.

A similar assessment can be made of the succeeding interwar period (1914–39), but there were some important differences. For one thing, agriculture became less important as a source of income to the middle class as a result of the Great Depression, while education became noticeably more important. Meanwhile, a new source of income growth arose, which had been of little significance before the First World War, namely industrialization. True, as a source of income and employment for the country as a whole, manufacturing industry remained limited, but it was no longer possible to ignore it as a source of income and wealth for the middle class as it had been before. With the exception of the inflationary war years, however, the rate of growth of income, and as a result the rate of social mobility, remained slow, which allows us to say that during the interwar years both the size and wealth of the Egyptian middle class remained, as it were, on the back burner.

It is not surprising, then, if our explanation is correct, to find that the cultural climate in Egypt remained refined throughout the 1920s and 1930s. This was the period that witnessed the major works of Taha Hussein, 'Abbas al-'Aqqad, Tawfik al-Hakim, Ahmad Amin, Salama Musa, Ibrahim al-Mazini, and so on. Egyptian poetry flourished under the pens of Ahmad Shawqi and Hafez Ibrahim, and music at the hands of Sayed Darwish, Zakariya Ahmad, and Muhammad al-Qasabgi. Theater advanced under the efforts of the likes of George Abiadh, Yusuf Wahbi, and Nagib al-Rihani, and the first Egyptian films appeared, some of them of an astonishingly high standard, including those produced by Egyptian women like 'Aziza Amir and

Fatma Rushdi. Sculpture underwent a revolution as seen in the works of Mahmud Mukhtar. The list goes on.

In 1914, some prominent Egyptian intellectuals formed a society called "The Committee of Writing, Translation, and Publishing," that was destined to play a magnificent role in spreading various branches of knowledge in Egypt and the Arab world. It went into decline after the end of the Second World War, and closed down completely at the end of the 1950s, leaving nothing behind but a printing press. The members of this society were of various specializations and different political and religious orientations, but they all shared a common trait, that of combining a high level of knowledge of Arab cultural heritage with an acquaintance of the latest developments of Western knowledge in one discipline or another, covering such a variety of subjects as astronomy, geography, chemistry, philosophy, history, literary criticism, and so on. By means of their intimate familiarity with classical Arabic literature, they were able to express their acquired knowledge of Western thought in polished Arabic, and if any of them translated a Western book of science or literature that fell within their area of expertise, the translation would usually turn out to be of the highest quality and clarity, sometimes attaining the level of literary writing. Many of those Egyptian intellectuals had been prepared for this happy combination of Arab and Western cultures through their study at the very fine "High School for Teacher Training," in which the students were thoroughly exposed to both traditions of knowledge.

\* \* \*

There occurred a noticeable decline in the quality of the dominant culture between the beginning of the Second World War and the July Revolution (1939–52). This again may be explained, at least partly, by the transformations that occurred in the middle class during that period. For one thing, this class grew substantially in size in response to the great amount of foreign expenditure to finance the war efforts, which, with the general scarcity of goods during the war, led to rampant inflation. New segments of the population were suddenly added to the old middle class, and enjoyed a sudden rise in wealth and social status without exerting much effort or engaging in really productive activity. These new segments may have constituted only a small percentage of the middle class, but the big increase in their purchasing power brought about a noticeable change in the country's cultural climate.

Toward the end of this period, the prominent playwright and novelist Tawfik al-Hakim published a short essay in the newspaper *Akhbar al-Yawm* (the publication of which was itself partly a reflection of this change of climate), entitled "The Age of Shukuku," which referred to the overwhelming success and wide popularity of the comedian Mahmud Shukuku. His was a new brand of monologue, employing short songs of light rhythm and humor. Using the expressions of the lower classes, he held up some of the abiding values of the old middle class to derision, and broke some of the old rules of classical song. He also brought a new feeling of intimacy to the bond between singers and audiences, relaxing the formality between them. These monologues, and those of others who achieved fame along with Mahmud Shukuku, responded to the tastes of the new wave of the *nouveaux riches*, who were more open to fun and satire than the existing members of the class they had recently joined, who tended to be more observant of older principles and traditions.

This period also witnessed a change in the music of Muhammad 'Abd al-Wahab, unanimously regarded as the greatest of twentieth-century Egyptian (and probably Arab) singers and composers, whose songs became faster in rhythm and shorter in length. His music became less observant of the strictures of classical Arabic music and his words closer to the language of the common people, but his songs also became less poetic than his own work of the 1920s and 1930s.

This was also the period in which a new voice in Egyptian journalism was heard, led by the publishing house of *Akhbar al-Yawm*, which was founded at the end of the war. It inaugurated a new school of Egyptian journalism, one based on sensationalism and news of crimes and scandals. It introduced large headlines and provocative images to attract the readership, and made more intensive use of humorous cartoons, which reflected the taste of a new audience more prepared to criticize and poke fun at established norms and the social values of the older middle class. Nevertheless, among the characters to appear frequently in the cartoons of this period was that of the "war profiteer," who was portrayed as grossly fat and ignorant, but able to spend profusely, as evidenced by the watch chain dangling from his pocket and the rings dripping from his fingers. Possessing no other virtue than that of extreme wealth, he lorded it over others simply because he had more ready money.

In the cinema and theater the works of Yusuf Wahbi and Nagib al-Rihani emphasized glaring class contradictions by showing a sharp contrast between the corrupt rich and the honest poor. There was also an increase in political violence, assassinations, and bombings in public places, especially by religious extremists, and a corresponding increase in the violence of the authorities' response to this. The great literary figures continued to write during the 1940s but they lost much of their vitality and enthusiasm for novelty and experimentation with their advancing years, while the new generation of writers did not demonstrate anything nearing the degree of seriousness and depth shown by the previous generation in their attempts to reconcile tradition with modernity.

When speaking of the cultural life of this period we should not close our eyes to the shift in the source of Western culture reaching Egypt, from Europe to America. The wave of westernization in Egyptian culture and social life that began at the beginning of the nineteenth century continued to emanate from Europe until the period now under discussion (1939–52), when it started to become increasingly American. This shift seemed to fit rather well with the higher rate of social mobility of the period in question, the greater value placed on wealth *per se*, with relatively little concern for the source of that wealth, and on the immediate enjoyment of life with less concern for the future, and with a weakening of the ties to the past and to historical roots.

Then came the revolution in 1952. It cannot be denied that a few years after the revolution, and largely because of it, Egypt entered an era that produced an intellectual climate of much finer quality than that which had prevailed during the war or in the years immediately following it. But it happened that in the succeeding two decades, the middle class grew at a rate even faster than that of the preceding period. More important were the new sources of the growth in the size and income of this class. There was an unprecedented expansion in education, with the removal of the barriers that had stood in the way of those who wished to receive an education in the 1930s and 1940s. The 1950s and 1960s also witnessed much more rapid industrialization, agricultural reform, and a growth in the armed forces, entailing increased utilities and public services. This also led to greater government intervention in economic and social life, which in turn led to further chances for advancement for the middle class, either through direct government employment or the growth of the private sector.

These sources of income growth in the two decades following the July Revolution were quite different in nature from those of the war years and the years immediately following the 1952–70 period. Now the sources of income were mainly productive services, in the sense that they

contributed to an increase in the nation's goods and services. Naturally there were examples of increases in
income and wealth that had come about without real
sacrifice or contribution to output, but these examples
were few and far between.

These new and mainly productive sources of income and
wealth were accompanied by a widespread optimism for
the social and political future of Egypt, while a genuine
sympathy on the part of most Egyptian intellectuals for the
social and political goals of the revolution contributed to
the vitality of the cultural climate of the day. Some of the
best works of Naguib Mahfouz and Yusuf Idris appeared in
this period, along with the most important plays of Nu'man
'Ashur, Alfred Farag, and Yusuf Idris. The period also witnessed the emergence of a new school of poetry led by
Salah 'Abd al-Sabur and 'Abd al-Mu'ti Higazi, and of the
brilliant colloquial poetry and caricatures of Salah Jahin,
and a new school of journalism led by Ahmad Baha' al-
Din. Meanwhile, Kamal al-Tawil, Baligh Hamdi, and
Muhammad al-Mugi composed fresh tunes to accompany
lyrics by talented songwriters that were more genuine and
optimistic in spirit than before. The songs were brought to
life by a voice that became immediately popular—that of
'Abd al-Halim Hafez. At the same time, Youssef Chahine
and Salah Abu Seif produced some of their greatest cine-
matic works.

In the following thirty years (1970–2000), numerous factors contributed to a deterioration in the quality of Egypt's

cultural climate in ways that would probably have been inconceivable to the authors of *On Egyptian Culture*, for it would seem that most of the things they complained about had now almost completely disappeared. It is true that some of the big names of the pre-1952 days continued to write in the same way and on the same subjects as they had before the revolution. The stories of Ihsan 'Abd al-Quddus and the plays of Tawfik al-Hakim, for instance, remained insensitive to the problems facing the majority of the population, while Naguib Mahfouz hardly changed course as a result of the revolution and his protagonists continued to be drawn from the narrow Cairene middle class, although in the 1960s, he took to writing stories of a more symbolic nature, behind which he concealed his dislike for the new regime. Aside from this, the general trend in literature, theater, cinema, and music was to open the door to the lower classes, by describing their problems and articulating their hopes and ambitions. The symptoms of cultural deterioration, therefore, have to be sought elsewhere.

We should note first of all the great and startling changes in the sources of income of the middle class as well as in the very size of the class itself. The rate of growth of the size of the middle class during the 1970s and 1980s was probably unprecedented in Egypt's modern history, but more important were the sources of this unprecedented growth. As I have tried to explain in my book *Whatever Happened to the Egyptians*, the major sources were migration and inflation, in addition to all kinds of intermediary services that grew in response to the launching of the open-door policy. This large and sudden increase in income and wealth was only weakly connected either to effort expended or to the level of education acquired, but it led to the inclusion of wide segments of society into the middle class, whose members were as little endowed with cultural sophistication as they were greatly endowed with purchasing power.

In addition to these three new sources of income and wealth, there were also important changes in two other sources of income for educated Egyptians, namely the Egyptian government and foreign institutions. With regard to the former, it was rather surprising that while the role of government in a variety of economic and social spheres declined noticeably, it actually increased in the area of culture, or at least in certain branches of culture. The sustained pressure on the government to open more schools and universities is understandable; what is harder to explain is the continued government involvement, perhaps to an even greater degree, in publishing books, newspapers, and magazines. In real terms, the state's support of the cinema and theater may have declined, but its expenditure on television most certainly had not.

Throughout the 1950s and 1960s the Egyptian government was naturally aware of the advantages of gaining the support of intellectuals and the educated elite for its policies. This was perfectly understandable from a government that had just laid the foundations for new foreign and domestic policies. In time, the government was expected to weaken its hold on intellectual activity as it weakened its hold on other aspects of life. This indeed was what happened with respect to its attitude toward the intellectuals of the opposition, who were no longer punished for expressing anti-government views. But this unfortunately was all there was to it, for the government never left the intellectuals alone.

From the mid-1970s, the government opened its coffers to anyone who was willing to promote its open-door policy, and its new stance toward Israel, the United States, and the Soviet Union. Indeed, President Sadat appeared more inclined throughout the 1970s to foster intellectuals than had 'Abd al-Nasser at any time in the 1950s and 1960s. Nasser in fact relied much more on the direct influence of his policies on the poor and middle classes who benefited from them, whereas Sadat was more in need of dressing up policies that were unpopular with both the masses and the intelligentsia.

But apart from the need to promote unpopular policies, there were other causes behind government intervention in cultural life during the 1970s and 1980s. The great expansion of education at all levels during the previous two decades, which emphasized quantity at the expense of quality of education, had created a new demand for various types of light culture and forms of entertainment that appealed to unsophisticated tastes and inclinations. These were easily accommodated by various forms of newspapers featuring sports, accidents, and crimes, but more especially by television programs, including rather shallow and simpleminded dramatic series and quiz shows. This kind of demand could of course have been easily met by the private sector. But for reasons of its own the government saw fit to answer much of the demand itself, by publishing new newspapers and magazines from the same publishing houses that it had established in the 1960s with entirely different goals. It also established broad-range television channels, and published large print-runs of cheaply priced books to appeal to a broad public. Were all of these outlets simply intended as pulpits for the propagation of government policies? Or were they for handing out some of the spoils of power to the heads of these government media enterprises? Whatever the real cause may be, publishing and broadcasting media are probably more completely controlled by the state today than they were at any time during the so-called socialist period.

There has also been an increase in the power of foreign influences, the most compelling of which have been those of the Gulf states, foreign companies, and international agencies. The Nasser regime of the 1950s and 1960s had placed strong impediments against such outside power by imposing high economic and political barriers against foreign companies and international financial institutions, and placing severe restrictions on migration to the Gulf. Perhaps these sources of foreign income were themselves too weak during Nasser's time to exercise any appreciable influence on the Egyptian cultural climate of the day. The Gulf states were unable to receive large numbers of Egyptian migrants before the rise in oil prices of 1973, and it was only in the mid-1970s that Egypt began its close relationship with the World Bank and the International Monetary Fund. The social and economic effects of this economic liberalization were of course more obvious than its cultural effects, but the latter were by no means insignificant. Although the combined effect of these domestic and external developments was not necessarily all negative, the resulting general intellectual climate has been quite dismal. The rapid growth of a middle class whose economic success derived largely from unproductive activities was combined with a rapid expansion of poor-quality education, and with a large role for a "soft" state that allowed a small number of individuals to exploit its resources for their own private gain. Besides the government, the influence of foreign companies and international organizations was also important, though mainly on research in social sciences and the humanities. For as they provided the funds to finance this research they also set its agenda and goals, even if these conflicted sharply with national priorities.

With greatly increased social mobility and the spread of education to various sectors of the population, it was natural that diverse talents in many fields of cultural endeavor should emerge in greater numbers than at mid-century, and indeed this is what happened in the realms of literature, theater, and film, as well as in economic, social, and political research. Therefore intellectual production was no longer confined, as it had been for many decades, to a few isolated oases in a vast arid desert, and the subjects tackled were no longer determined by the inclinations of a small number of talented individuals belonging to a highly privileged class. What had been the main cause of the complaint of the authors of *On Egyptian Culture* was no longer relevant, with talents emerging from a great variety of income groups, in all fields of intellectual life, and in every subject of inquiry. No longer can anyone complain that entire classes are deprived of giving expression to their problems and aspirations. Rather, the problem has now become the sharp competition between one mode of cultural production, enjoying a large demand and state support, and another mode, of higher quality and nobler purposes, but deprived of both sufficient funding and the support of the state.

As an example, consider a strange phenomenon that was hardly known in the 1950s and 1960s but which has become quite common in Egyptian journalism: the occupation of regular column space in government-owned newspapers and magazines by writers with very limited talent or popularity. Week after week, such writers impose themselves on readers for no other reason than their ability, by one means or another, to insinuate themselves into the favor of the officials at these press outlets.

This kind of "success," based purely on contacts, could not happen in the theater or cinema, which in contrast to government-owned newspapers rely upon popular acceptance for box office success. In this case the lowbrow work that drives out the good cannot be entirely devoid of public appeal. Instead, the shrinking of the role of government in supporting highbrow theater and film production has left the field wide open for the exploitation of sex or buffoonery.

Indeed, the use of sex to sell magazines and newspapers has become noticeably widespread over the last ten years in a way unknown in any previous period in the history of the Egyptian press. Some of the venerable political magazines have resorted to the same strategy in order to attract more readers, especially since the appeal of political stories has declined for reasons beyond their control.

A similar thing has happened with music and song, although the use of sex has been inevitably less obvious here than in journalism. Nevertheless it can be felt in the types of compositions, the arrangements, the lyrics, the tone of the singer's voice, and, even, in the actual appearance of the singers, who now rely more on their looks than ever before. This has given rise to a new genre of song called the "youth song," which holds little appeal to audiences over forty, who still find comfort in more old-fashioned types of singing. In fact these "old-fashioned" types do not go back very far in history, but include many songs from the 1950s and 1960s.

A similar development occurred even in the field of religious writing, where once again the lowbrow has driven out the good. This becomes particularly evident if we compare the writings of recent years with those of the first half of the twentieth century. I am referring particularly to the

120

highly irrational interpretations of religion that have gained widespread popularity through radio, television, and the press, where the emphasis is placed on outward appearances of religiosity as opposed to the true spirit of a religion and its higher goals. This trend includes attaching significance to the resemblance between some of the expressions used in religious texts and those of modern science, the implication being that these texts had already anticipated modern scientific discoveries. Added to this has been the tendency to drag religion more and more into social and political issues.

Literary writing and criticism have been afflicted by two new phenomena that may appear at first to be completely separate, but actually reflect the same characteristics of the new cultural climate. The first is the oft-repeated tendency of writers of novels and short stories to show deliberate disrespect to religion in a way that was unacceptable and indeed unimaginable a few decades ago. The second is the appearance of works of literature that are beyond the level of comprehension of most readers. If some readers are bold enough to criticize these works, the authors themselves or professional literary critics jump to their defense, claiming that these are great works, despite their abstruseness, as they belong to the modern or postmodern school of literature, and only the initiated or those of a sufficiently refined education can deconstruct their symbolism. These two new phenomena may have one important thing in common, namely a strong inclination to imitate certain fashionable trends in the West.

A parallel development occurred in the fields of social research. Since the mid-1970s, the number of grants and various other types of support offered by international and other foreign institutions to Egyptian scholars in the fields of social science and the humanities have multiplied. Little wonder that the subjects that have attracted the greatest attention from Egyptian researchers are the subjects that were particularly favored by these institutions, such as women's liberation, humans rights, democracy, the state of ethnic and religious minorities, and the advantages of privatization or structural reform, including the liberalization of foreign trade, the encouragement of foreign investment, and the reduction of the role of the state in the economy.

It is unfortunate, but not surprising, under the influence of all of these factors, that the role of the state has turned little by little away from supporting a high-quality culture and attempting to shield the public from a deluge of commercialism to exactly the opposite. It is sad to see Egyptian state-owned television, for example, being governed increasingly by the profit motive, submitting more and more with each passing day to the demands of advertisers, or to see government publishing houses succumbing to the interests of influential persons motivated mainly by the acquisition of wealth or power, or to see the most prestigious of state prizes governed increasingly by the same interests.

* * *

To summarize, all of the following factors have worked together to produce the prevailing cultural climate in Egypt: a sudden and undiscriminating opening up to Western economic and cultural influences; a high rate of migration to the oil-rich Gulf states; steep rises in the inflation rate; a wide expansion in education concomitant with a noticeable decline in its quality; a rapid growth of the middle class combined with a widening disparity between income earned and the effort expended in securing it, along with the rapid accumulation of wealth by new segments of society with less sophisticated tastes and little or no education; the increased penetration by foreign companies into Egyptian economic life with a concomitant increase in the activity of foreign and international cultural and financial institutions in financing social research. Combined with all of this has been the evolution of the role of the Egyptian state, which, while relinquishing many of its former responsibilities in the economic and social spheres, has maintained its control over cultural institutions and the mass media.

The result is a cultural climate noticeably different from that of fifty years ago. The main issue of that time was the apparent indifference shown by the great writers of the day to problems arising from the class struggle and the large divide between socio-economic classes. This is not how it can be characterized now. Instead, the issue has become that of an uneven struggle between a culture that is largely in the service of commercial interests, both foreign and domestic, backed by huge resources as well as by the authority of the state, and another type of culture that is far more sophisticated, with nobler motives, and which is far more sensitive to the needs of most Egyptians, of whatever class.

# 10

## The Economy

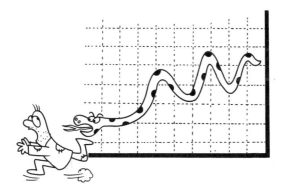

Seen from an economist's point of view, the fifty years since the July Revolution may be divided into two periods, which by pure coincidence are of roughly equal length. During those two periods Egypt witnessed two entirely different orientations of economic policy: one in which the state interfered mightily in economic life, and the other coming very close to a free economy. The date that divides the two periods is not the death of 'Abd al-Nasser in 1970, but the inauguration of the open-door policy (or *infitah*) in 1974. Hence, each of the two systems prevailed for about a quarter-century, and it is important to compare the fruits of the two systems. This is what I have tried to do here. Some of the results may surprise some readers, and may upset the partisans of one system or the other.

In the mid-twentieth century, Egypt could be cited as an excellent example of what in those days was called an "underdeveloped" country, but it was also an overpopulated country. Egypt's population was then about twenty million people, of whom some 80 percent were making a living in agriculture, although the amount of arable land had increased negligibly since the beginning of the century. The average annual per capita income at mid-century was equivalent to less than one hundred U.S. dollars, but aside from this already low average, the distribution of national income among the population was extremely uneven, such that more than 80 percent were making far less than one hundred dollars a year.

It was obvious, then, that economic reform required three basic things: the growth of national income at a rate higher than that of the population, a change in the economic structure so as to create jobs in sectors other than agriculture, especially in manufacturing, and a more equitable distribution of income guaranteeing the fulfillment of the basic needs of the population, such as an adequate level of food consumption, clothing, shelter, education, health services, and so on.

During the two decades following the 1952 revolution (1952–74), the Egyptian government tried to achieve these three goals, not by relying on free market forces, but through direct intervention in various aspects of economic and social life. The most important of these were successive agricultural reforms starting in 1952, and the Egyptianization and nationalization of all large (and not so large) industrial firms, all banks and insurance companies, and a great number of trade and service establishments. A system of central planning was adopted, involving forceful intervention in foreign trade, investment, employment, and price determination, as well as the provision of many basic services at heavily subsidized prices, including education, healthcare, and housing.

Egypt was by no means the only example at the time of far-reaching government intervention in economic and social life. It was a common phenomenon in that period in many Third World countries, and even to a noticeable degree in industrialized countries. This is not difficult to explain. Many Third World countries had gained their political independence right after the end of the Second World War, and the reins of government were taken over by national leaders who had earned wide popular support for their struggle to gain that independence. Who could the people have trusted more to fulfill the next important goals of rapid economic development and greater social justice?

But this was also the period (1952–73) that saw the greatest popularity in the West for Keynesian economics, which lent additional support to interventionist government economic policy. It was the same period that saw a large increase in the amount of foreign aid granted by the more developed to the less developed countries. This consisted largely of official aid granted by governments, state agen-

127

cies, or international institutions to Third World governments for financing development projects. It seemed natural that the governments of developing countries receiving that aid should also be the ones to implement these projects. The Cold War, which allowed many Third World governments a relatively high degree of freedom vis-à-vis the two superpowers, and the early success of Soviet comprehensive planning in accelerating industrialization, must also have given additional support to the philosophy of central planning and a prominent role for government. What were the results of this as far as Egypt was concerned?

The results for income growth were as excellent in the first half of that period (1952–65) as they were disappointing in the second (1965–75). If one were to ignore the first three or four years after the revolution (1952–56), when the government was more concerned with politics than with economics, leaving the economy to proceed in the same old way of pre-revolutionary years, the rate of growth increased dramatically from the mid-1950s, and remained vigorous until the end of the first five-year plan in the mid-1960s. Real per capita income increased at an average rate of between three and 4 percent per year for a period of ten years, so that between 1955 and 1965 real per capita income rose by about 50 percent, which was by the standards of the day a very satisfactory achievement. After that, however, per capita income almost stagnated until the mid-1970s. It is safe to say, therefore, that in the entire period from 1952 to 1975, real per capita income showed a moderate increase of between 50 and 60 percent.

The achievements of the revolutionary government were much more impressive with regard to the other two goals, namely the change in economic structure and income redistribution. There is no doubt that by 1975 Egypt had become more of an industrial nation than it had been in 1952—the share of manufacturing in the gross national product at the end of the period being far greater than it had been at the beginning. Similarly the distribution of national income had become much more equitable in 1975 than it had been in 1952. Egyptian society had become much less polarized, and the relative size of the middle class had grown noticeably larger than it had been on the eve of the revolution.

This trend went into sharp reversal in the mid-1970s. It did not happen overnight, but we did wake up every day to find some new retrenchment of the accomplishments of the 1950s and 1960s. In agriculture, not only was there no further advance in land reform, but the government gradually withdrew the protection it formerly extended to tenants against landlords. Government subsidies were gradually reduced or abolished, and nationalized establishments were privatized one after another. Imports were liberalized, and so, to some extent, was the exchange rate, while tax rates on income and wealth were sharply reduced, and new laws passed to grant much greater concessions to foreign investors.

These changes in Egypt's economic policy, when taken as a whole, amounted to no less than another revolution in

Egypt's economic system. From the mid-1970s on, the "open-door economy" became the sign of the times, by whatever name it may be called—open-door, economic reform, structural adjustment, and so on.

However, what happened to economic policy in Egypt in the mid-1970s must be seen as part of a worldwide phenomenon. Rather than viewing this change as the result of some bright idea on the part of the Egyptian president or one of his principal advisers at the time, it is much more likely to have been the result of the changing international climate with or without—but most probably with—some measure of external pressure. But whatever may have been the cause, the results were quite dramatic.

From 1975 to the present, the growth of per capita income followed a pattern very similar to that of the previous period: a high rate of growth in the first ten years, followed by virtual stagnation in the next ten years. In the decade from 1975 to 1985, Egypt witnessed an average growth rate of GDP that was almost unprecedented in the whole of Egypt's economic history during the twentieth century, permitting an average annual increase in real per capita income of between 5 and 6 percent. This was followed by very low growth rates between the mid-1980s and the early 1990s, and the situation did not get much better as the 1990s wore on. Thus it may be said that in the final quarter of the century (1975–2000), real per capita income nearly doubled, but that most of that increase occurred in the first ten years of that period.

This rise in average income achieved during the period of the open-door economy was significantly greater than that achieved with a much greater dose of government intervention over the previous quarter-century. Nevertheless, the open-door period was far worse than the previous period with respect to the other two goals, namely changing the economic structure and income redistribution.

As far as the economic structure is concerned, the share of manufacturing in GNP, total wages, and in total exports is now smaller than it was in 1965, while the share of oil, tourism, and remittances from laborers working abroad has increased. As for income distribution, it is now much less equitable than it was in 1975. Egyptian society may have come to deserve to be called a society of two nation, now more than at any other time since, and perhaps even before, the revolution.

From this brief survey of Egyptian economic development over the last fifty years, the reader may feel inclined to conclude that the Egyptian experience during this period merely lends support to the widely-held belief that open-door policies are good for growth but not necessarily for income distribution or for improving the economic structure. On the other hand, while a big dose of government intervention may improve income distribution, accelerate economic diversification, and raise the rate of industrialization, at least for a while, it must slow down the rate of growth in the long run.

The fact is that many advocates of the open-door policy

in Egypt are willing to admit that this policy has hampered an equitable distribution of income, but they are quick to add that the benefits such a policy is bound to produce will in the long run trickle down to the poor. They are much less ready to admit that the policy of large-scale government intervention is more effective than the free market in raising the rate of industrialization. Rather, they are inclined to attribute the open-door policy's failure to increase the rate of industrialization to exactly the opposite reason, namely to Egypt's failure to accelerate its adoption of free-market policies.

On the other hand, many of the advocates of a larger role for government are prepared to admit that open-door policies have raised the rate of income growth, but that this was achieved at the expense of a more equitable distribution of income, greater economic independence, and an improved economic structure. Moreover, they reject the assertion that the increase in the rate of growth of national income associated with economic liberalization can persist in the long run.

So, each side is convinced that the policy it advocates is the better for the long run in these three areas: a higher rate of income growth, faster industrialization, and a more equitable distribution of income. Such a dispute may appear odd to a natural scientist, who sees economists unable to agree on such a simple though vital issue, namely whether or not government intervention is better for the economy than the free play of market forces. At the same time, a natural scientist may also be surprised at the degree of confidence with which an economist may be willing to ascribe the success or failure of economic performance to one specific economic policy instead of another, when so many other factors may have interfered either to strengthen or nullify the effect of a particular policy.

Thus in Egypt, for instance, the past fifty years have borne witness to enormously important developments besides those that took place with respect to the state's role in the economy, which must themselves have had far-reaching effects on income distribution, rates of growth, or economic structure. It would seem rash, therefore, to try to defend a particular economic policy simply by looking at what happened to these three basic economic indicators.

In fact, the development of these three indicators in Egypt over the past 50 years seems to have been largely determined by purely external factors. Favorable effects on the performance of the Egyptian economy may have had little to do with the type of economic policy being implemented. For example, the Cold War of the 1950s and 1960s had an important beneficial effect on economic performance in Egypt, in that it allowed large amounts of foreign aid with lenient conditions to flow to Egypt from both camps. The rise in oil prices in 1973–74 and again in 1979–80 also had an important positive effect on economic performance, not just because of the increased revenues from oil exports, but also, more importantly, because of the increased demand for Egyptian labor in the oil-rich Gulf states and Libya. This led to greatly increased labor remittances, which contributed not just to a higher rate of growth, but also to a mitigation of the disparity in income distribution.

On the discouraging side there were also important external factors at play that led to the deterioration in economic performance, regardless of which policy was in place. There was, for instance, a large drop in oil prices in 1986, as well as what is commonly referred to as "terrorist" activities that led every now and again to large decreases in the revenues from tourism. But most important of all was the 1967 war, which caused the loss of oil revenues from Sinai, the closure of the Suez Canal, and the virtual disappearance of revenues from tourism. All of this led to a large decrease in Egypt's proceeds of foreign exchange and a severe reduction in investment, which in turn led to a fall in the rate of industrialization, and indeed to the inability of the government to pursue its policy of income redistribution.

What does all this mean? It means that it is difficult to identify economic success or failure with the adoption of one economic system rather than another, and that we may have greatly exaggerated, for purely ideological reasons, the impact of economic philosophy on economic performance.

History is full of examples of successful economic performance under strict government control, and just as full of successful examples under a fairly free market system. Egypt's economic history provides examples of both types of success or failure. For successful economic performance under strict government control, Egypt offers the two examples of development under Muhammad 'Ali in the first decades of the nineteenth century, and under 'Abd al-Nasser in the middle of the twentieth. But Egypt also witnessed rapid growth with improvement in income distribution in the first decade of economic liberalization (1975–85), albeit for reasons other than economic liberalization. Poor performance was also experienced under strict government control (1965–75) as well as under a much freer economy (1985–95).

What the Egyptian experience in economic development over the last fifty years does show, as I am sure do the experiences of many other countries, is that the degree of foreign pressure to which a country is subjected and its levels of internal corruption are far more decisive influences on its economic performance than the nature of its economic system, since a high degree of foreign pressure or corruption could prevail as much under a system of heavy government intervention as it could in a free market system.[15]

# 11

## Rich and Poor

One of Marxism's famous tenets is that the state is primarily a tool used by the privileged classes to subjugate other classes. So there is no such thing in the Marxist scheme of things as a neutral state with respect to class struggle. Anyone who thinks that the state could act as a referee between classes or that it might be possible to persuade it to act on behalf of the underprivileged at the expense of the privileged is a dreamer. This means that political power must sooner or later redound to those who possess economic power. So if one class rises to the point where it attains greater economic power, it must also ultimately rise to attain greater political influence. This idea has much to recommend it. History has provided many examples of its veracity, and common sense lends it much support.

Take for example a society that relies heavily on agriculture, and consists of a very small proportion of rich landowners, and a vast majority, upward of 80 percent, of poor farmers, most of whom are living at subsistence level. In this situation, the state must protect the large landowners against any hostility that might be shown by the poor. At the same time, the state must undertake certain projects, such as the construction and maintenance of irrigation and drainage canals necessary for the continuation and increase of agricultural production, the benefit of which will accrue mainly to the landowners. The only source of finance for such projects is agricultural rent, as the wages of the agricultural laborers and the income of the tenants are far too low to allow for tax deduction. A tax on the rent received by the big landlords must be the main source of state income, but the state spends the tax revenue on projects that are of primary benefit to those same landlords.

This was in general outline the role assumed by the state in Egypt prior to the revolution of 1952. The state kept the peace, maintained law and order, and protected the rich, the great majority of whom were large landowners. Economic policy was almost entirely confined to maintaining, and, when possible, to increasing agricultural production. The main source of state finance, apart from customs duties, was the "land tax," which was significantly called *al-mal* ("the money"), paid by the large landowners, but from which the smallholders were exempt.

The 1952 revolution began by banishing this rich landowning class from political power through a series of land reform laws and successive measures of sequestration and confiscation. The machinery of power passed to segments of the middle class, or, to be more precise, those segments of the population that constituted the middle class at the time of the revolution, and consisted mainly of professionals of all types such as engineers, lawyers, managers, accountants, teachers, government officials, army officers as well as a small class of middle-income landowners. These groups had been almost completely excluded from the exercise of power before the revolution, or indeed from wielding any wide influence at all. The revolution accorded this class a chance to rise both economically and politically. Political and economic power were quickly reunited within a very short time after the revolution, just as they had been before it. And the state oriented its laws and policies toward serving this newly rich and powerful class according to the same general law: the state is always at the service of the economically privileged class.

There can be no doubt that one of the most important results of the July Revolution was the replacement of one social class by another in the position of economic and political advantage. Indeed it could be argued that this is the main justification for calling the events of July 1952 a "revolution." It must, however, be admitted that wide segments of the Egyptian population, those belonging to much lower income groups, have also realized important benefits from the revolution in the form of free education and highly subsidized essential goods and services such as basic foodstuffs, health services, housing, and transportation. New employment opportunities at fairly decent wages were created for members of the lower income groups, who also benefited from guaranteed government jobs on finishing their school years. Nevertheless, it can safely be said that during the 1950s and 1960s most of the benefits of the government's new investments and public expenditure went to the new class in power, namely the new middle class. This can be seen in investment policies favoring the production of goods and services that were affordable only by this class and which were beyond the reach of a good proportion—say 40 percent or more—of the population. Examples include the establishment of industries producing air conditioners, refrigerators, or private cars, the construction and development of summer resorts, new social and sporting clubs and new residential districts for new upper-middle class families, among whom army officers have often been particularly privileged.

The driving forces behind this increase in consumption during the 1950s and 1960s were the new development projects in industry, agriculture, and services. These included new factories of all kinds, the Aswan High Dam, and many large projects for increasing electricity supply, upgrading means of transportation, and the building of new schools and hospitals, and so on.

Who put up the money for all this? The old rich had been stricken; they scarcely had the resources to finance such projects, while the state had neither the ideology nor the requisite cruelty, as did the Soviet state, for instance, to extract any surplus from the lower social classes or the small landowners and their tenants, who benefited from land redistribution and the fixing of rents. To finance this development the revolutionary government resorted to external sources, either through the nationalization of foreign assets inside of Egypt (such as the Suez Canal or foreign banks and insurance companies), or through foreign loans. It is probably safe to say that it was that sizable flow of foreign resources into Egypt that enabled the Egyptian state in the 1950s and 1960s to show such generosity toward the lowest classes on the social ladder, without at the same time granting them any real say in the affairs of state. Meanwhile, the lion's share of the country's wealth had, of course, to continue to fall into the lap of the class that did hold such power.

If this class analysis comes close to the truth for Egypt of the 1950s and 1960s, it must be even closer to the truth for the three succeeding decades. For after a few grim years of economic stagnation (1967–75), during which those external sources had virtually dried up, new sources of income, also external, emerged during the following ten years (1975–85) allowing almost everyone to take a place at the banquet. These new sources included remittances from Egyptians working abroad; foreign aid now given generously as a reward for Egypt in return for the radical reorientation of its foreign and economic policies; windfall revenues from oil exports as a result of the large increase in oil prices in 1973–74 following the October

War, and again in 1979, following the revolution in Iran; Suez Canal revenues after its reopening in 1975; as well as the increase in revenues from tourism. This was the period when Egypt realized the unprecedented rate of growth in GDP of 8 percent or more already referred to in the previous chapter, that allowed those who were already well-off to realize unprecedented increases in wealth, but also allowed the previously less wealthy to join the ranks of the rich. It also permitted a significant increase in the standard of living for broad segments of the lower classes who benefited from the new opportunities opened up through migration.

Did the Egyptian state continue to serve the interests of the privileged classes? Yes, of course, and in a manner that had probably been unknown in Egypt since the time of Muhammad 'Ali. The late president Anwar al-Sadat would boast publicly that during his reign, the wealth of the rich multiplied several times as a result of the several-fold increase in the value of real estate. Indeed, he was inclined to use this as a measure of the success of his economic policies. More and more, the *nouveaux riches*, who had gained the upper hand in business and construction contracting, were drawn to his administration, while it became quite common for the offspring of politically important people to engage themselves in the import/export trade (doing more importing than exporting). With extraordinary ease they obtained the necessary authorizations and licenses to operate and get rich quickly by procuring building materials at subsidized prices, customs exemptions, or by buying government-owned real estate at very attractive prices, and so on.

The inflation rate in that period reached an unusually high level for Egypt of more than 20 percent per year. The *nouveaux riches* benefited greatly from this, and none but a small portion of the population was harmed by it, specifically people on fixed incomes, since migration for work and the flow of wealth from all sides allowed the great majority of the population to increase its income.

A radical change occurred around the time of the mid-1980s. While the state continued to function at the service of the rich, something else happened to darken the picture considerably. For the rate of growth in national income declined sharply as a result of several interrelated factors: a steep decline in oil prices; a sharp reduction in the numbers of workers migrating abroad, and even a net inflow of migrants to Egypt; the adoption by the government of severe deflationary measures in accordance with the directives of the International Monetary Fund; and violent fluctuations in tourism revenues. The result of all this was that the last fifteen years of the century (1985–2000) were marked by a severe decline in the rate of income growth to almost half the level of the previous decade and a large increase in the rate of unemployment, particularly among university graduates.

Under such circumstances, one might have expected that the cost of such a general decline in economic conditions would be borne by everyone, rich and poor alike. But such an outcome would have been too simple, for what happened ultimately depended on the capacity of each segment of the population to resist a decline in its living standard, or even to raise it, if at all possible, and if need be at the expense of others. Those with a large capacity for such resistance were inevitably those closest to the holders of the reigns of power, and it is they who, even under conditions of severe depression, can realize some net gain and add to their already high incomes and wealth. But in conditions of very low growth of total income, the price that has to be paid for this by the rest of the population is inevitably high.

This is exactly what happened in the last fifteen years of the twentieth century, and it amounted to no less than a transfer of income from the poor to the rich. Such was, for instance, the net impact of the newly imposed sales tax, the burden of which falls more heavily on the poor than on the rich, while state-owned land continued to be sold to the rich at less than its real value. Such, too, was the net impact of huge bank loans being handed out to borrowers of dubious reputation, who made use of their personal connections with those in power to deposit the proceeds abroad. In all these methods of income transfer from poor to rich, the role of the state is clearly vital. The Marxist view of the state seems, in Egypt's case at least, to have been vindicated.

# 12

## The Circus

When the idea of a national circus was suggested to Gamal 'Abd al-Nasser in 1960 as part of a five-year cultural plan, he saw nothing wrong with it, and so the idea was put into practice, and the circus was opened in 1966 in the neighborhood of Agouza on the west bank of the Nile. The idea was that the state would support the venerable circus that the Helw family had established at the dawn of the twentieth century and had continued to direct and perform in for generations. The state would spend on the circus to develop and modernize it and establish a permanent home for it in a purpose-built big top.

It was a good idea. No one could gainsay it. The circus is an ancient art form, known in one form or another in diverse cultures of every age. In it, seemingly ordinary people, by virtue of sheer sharp-wittedness and courage, appear to perform miracles, taming wild animals, and molding the human body at will as though it were a lump of clay, making it appear by turns as light as feather and as hard as steel, or tempering and playing with fire as though it were cool and safe. Thus the circus has come to be a unique source of enjoyment and excitement to audiences of all ages and from every walk of life.

The opening of the National Circus was part of a successful attempt to spark a general cultural renaissance in Egypt. This was part of a wider scheme which included, among other things, theater, ballet, folk art, and classical and Arab music institutes, and it succeeded in unearthing new talent and in attracting wide audiences, until the events of 1967 put an end to it.

Soon after the military attack against Egypt and the Israeli occupation of Sinai, the National Circus suffered a recession, as did many other aspects of life in Egypt. This derived as much from the depression and hopelessness felt by many Egyptians in the wake of the army's rout at the hands of the Israeli army, as from any reduction in spending. It was not expected, then, in the years following the disaster of 1967 that the National Circus would continue in its former brilliance, or that the performers would perform with the same high spirits and dedication, or even that the audiences would attend with the same level of enthusiasm as before.

In this general, dispiriting climate, a tragic accident befell the most important personality of the circus and the most prominent member of the Helw family. A lion named Sultan fatally mauled the trainer Muhammad Helw as he stood in the ring before the audience. This was on the night of October 12, 1972, and it so happened, that the gifted Egyptian author Yusuf Idris was in the audience that night. In the tremendous shock of the event, Idris saw something fearsome in the human side of the tragedy, symbolizing not only the state of the circus at the time, but also the political and social life of Egypt in the aftermath of the Israeli attack. He recorded his impressions in a famous essay entitled, "I am Sultan, the Law of the Jungle," which he published in the newspaper *Al-Ahram* a few days later. The essay had widespread reverberations of its own, because it echoed exactly what many people were feeling at the time. He concluded that the lion's attack on the trainer was an allegory for the state of Egyptians of that time– fearful, defeated, their high ideals lost, and their dreams of heroism and glory destroyed.

It has been over thirty years since that event and the publication of the essay in question. Many things have happened in Egypt since, and the Egypt of 2002 is not the Egypt of 1972. The 1973 war broke out, then peace ensued. Difficult economic times came and went, only to return once more. Tourism flourished several times and then collapsed several times. Millions traveled to the Gulf and millions came home again. Unemployment eased considerably and then flared up with a vengeance. But something just as important arose then that remains to this day, and that is the weakness that has stricken the state.

For one reason or another, the Egyptian state has been afflicted by a disease that may be called "a softening of the bones." After playing such an important role in the economic and social life that led to a great reduction in inequality, the state gradually withdrew from one type of activity after another, leaving the door wide open to plunder by a small class of people who happened to enjoy some political or economic privileges. The gap between rich and poor began to grow again after two decades of economic policies aimed at bringing them closer together, so that by the end of the century, Egypt came to deserve, probably even more than it had just before the 1952 revolution, to be called a country of two nations, a phrase which Disraeli used to describe the England of 150 years ago. [16] The divide is not merely an economic one, but one of sentiments, aspirations, and lifestyles as well.

This alarming divide affected many aspects of social life in Egypt, including the National Circus. The circus remains under the purview of the Ministry of Culture, and those who work in it are employees of that ministry. But the Ministry of Culture has itself become two ministries, just as Egypt has become two nations. There is the grand ministry known to the upper class of culture consumers, which includes such things as the opera house, the splendid conferences of the High Council for Culture, exhibitions of paintings and sculpture presided over by the minister, as well as the occasional performance of Verdi's *Aida* in Luxor or the New Year's Eve festivals at the pyramids. At the other end of the scale, there is the Cairo International Book Fair, which has become a promenade for the masses who can afford the half-pound price of admission, and who, once inside, can find relatively cheap books and sandwiches. And there is also the National Circus.

When Yusuf Idris wrote about his impressions of the circus in 1972, he had already noted the signs of poverty and neglect that had begun to appear in the clothes worn by the performers, and the platforms that they stood on. Today the neglect and complete lack of care show in everything, from the bleachers for the audience to the tattered circus tent that lets in the cold air of a winter's night, compelling some spectators to leave with their children before the end of a show. This is not to mention the embarrassingly low salaries earned by the artists: the most daring and skillful among them might earn 250 Egyptian pounds a month, or less than US\$50, a part of which they must use to buy their own costumes.

But the circus itself is again divided into two nations: at the very top, there is the Helw family who started the circus a hundred years ago and who leases the circus to the government through a private company; meanwhile, in the ring sits a humble workman called Suleiman 'Ashur Suleiman, fifty-three years of age, who has been working in the circus since he was twenty, and whose monthly salary is still a meager 100 Egyptian pounds. As a result, he has never been able to marry, and to save money, he sleeps on the ground between the animal cages.

There must be millions of men like Suleiman 'Ashur Suleiman in Egypt today, but few of them will have had an experience as horrifying as that which befell the handler Suleiman on January 4, 2002. After the performance had ended on that night, Suleiman 'Ashur and his colleagues began driving the animals back into their cages. For some reason or another Suleiman decided to walk on some of the cages, one of which belonged to a tiger named Muhsin. Accounts of exactly what happened next differ; it is said that one of his legs slipped between the bars of the cage within easy reach of the tiger, who grabbed it and bit it. It is also said, and this seems more plausible, that the tiger reached out of the cage and caught Suleiman by his shoe, dragged his leg into the cage, and then bit him.

Suleiman was taken to hospital, where his leg was amputated. When the news reached the papers, people who had previously never taken any notice of Suleiman 'Ashur learned that in Egypt there could still be someone who had been working for thirty-three years in such a poorly-paid and dangerous job, earning just 100 pounds a month, with no pension or retirement benefits and no health insurance.

The people of Egypt took old Uncle Suleiman to their hearts, and large numbers of people, great and small, went to visit him in hospital. Famous artists and ordinary people left him sums of money in envelopes without leaving their names. No one was surprised to find him patiently

150

submissive to the will of Allah, looking upon what had happened to him as ineluctable fate. What they did find strange was that the only thing worrying him was that the circus might dispense with his services after the loss of his leg. He kept mentioning it over and over again to anyone who visited him, as if he were asking for their help in realizing his hope of returning to work.

It is difficult to resist reading the two awful incidents of the lion Sultan and the tiger Muhsin, separated by thirty years, as symbols of an important change that had overcome Egyptians in the meantime. Thirty years ago, Egyptians were suffering from a black depression and loss of confidence brought on by the Israeli attack of 1967 and the occupation of Sinai. This was what Yusuf Idris evoked in his description of the attack by the lion Sultan against the trainer Muhammad Helw. In Idris's view, the lion had only intended to inspire in Muhammad Helw his old enthusiasm, boldness, and self- confidence. So he tried at first to make him angry by brandishing his paw at him as though he meant to attack him. But when he saw the fear on the face of Muhammad Helw and saw him take a step backward, the lion himself grew angry and snapped at him, killing him. It never crossed the lion's mind that his action would kill his beloved trainer. He was only trying to return him to his old state. The lion himself slipped into a deep depression, stopped eating, and died a few days later.

The situation with the handler Suleiman and the tiger Muhsin was very different. It had nothing to do with courage, fear, or feelings of hope or despair. Instead, it revolved around one thing: hunger. The handler was hungry and the tiger was hungry, and so, it seems, is a good proportion of the Egyptian population.

This state of hunger was made clear in the information about the circus published in the papers after the incident. The circus had about twenty lions and tigers, each one of them requiring about twenty-five kilograms of meat a day. The circus administration buys that much meat each day, and in order to cut costs it does not always buy the required buffalo or beef, but buys some donkey meat a few days a week, which is much cheaper. But feeding lions and tigers on donkey meat is not without its risks, since this meat has a higher sugar content than beef or buffalo, making it closer in taste to human flesh. So accustoming lions and tigers to a diet of donkey meat can make them hungry for human flesh.

In light of this, is it possible that the explanation for what happened between Suleiman the handler and Muhsin the tiger is that someone decided to save money by feeding the beast donkey meat, or that the person responsible for feeding the tiger had filched some of the tiger's ration for himself?

This could be the reason why the tiger seized the handler by his foot and dragged him toward the cage, if that is indeed what happened. Even if the alternative story were true, a man slipping his leg into a tiger's cage should not be thought of as something normal. It is not something to be expected, unless the handler was not himself in good shape, which might make him more likely to lose his balance, or take no notice of the danger he is in, or do something stupid like run along the tops of the cages instead of walking between them. Any one of these things is more likely to happen with a hungry man. And why should we find it strange that the handler Suleiman, with his miserable salary, was indeed a hungry man?

Of course hunger is by no means limited to the handler Suleiman and the tiger Muhsin alone. At least half the employees of the Ministry of Culture must suffer from hunger of some kind. We mustn't let ourselves be fooled by the name of the ministry they work for and assume that all the people who work there are occupied only with cultural interests, and that such a preoccupation banishes hunger pangs. Remember that the ministry is riven in two, thereby mirroring Egyptian society as a whole. There must be thousands who fall into the culture ministry's second division: the people who sell the books in its bookstores, for example, or transfer the books from storage, or drive the ministry cars, or keep the culture palaces in Cairo and its environs clean. This reckons without those employees at the circus who drive the animals from their cages into the ring and back, or prepare their feed, or clean their cages, and so on. A high proportion of these people must be suffering from hunger in one form or another, or at least from the fear of hunger, like Suleiman the handler, who was gripped by the fear that he may not be able to return to his work.

# 13

---

# A Train Journey

Even though the people who ride in the third-class carriages of Egyptian trains, and the people who take the
minibuses between Cairo and Alexandria, or between
regional towns and villages make up, together with their
families, more than half the Egyptian people, the Egyptian
media, nevertheless, has almost nothing to say about them.
If you only get your information from Egyptian radio and
television, and Egyptian newspapers and magazines, whatever their political orientation, you will not learn any but
the most superficial news about the way of life of those
passengers. It is true that some news about them may
appear on the so-called "regional news" pages of some
newspapers or the "news of the governorates" sections

(which refer to all the governorates of Egypt other than those of Cairo and Alexandria), but the greater part of these news stories address either the activities of the governor and his associates or the projects that the ministry of agriculture is planning to implement, with only the rarest mention of the issues that are of real concern to those people who make up the majority of the Egyptian population. It is also true that the accident pages carry news almost every day of the accidents that befall the taxis and microbuses that ply the roads between the small towns and villages, but these stories usually only list the impersonal detail of the incidents: the numbers injured, the time of the accident, the license plates of the vehicles involved, and what the police did or are planning to do about what happened.

That whole routine changed as a result of the disaster that befell southbound train number 832 traveling from Cairo to Aswan on the night of Tuesday, February 19, 2002, and early the following Wednesday morning. Faced with a disaster of this magnitude, which took the lives of hundreds of people, it was impossible for the media to keep quiet about the people on the last seven cars of the train, all of whom were third class passengers, especially as the world press had gotten wind of the event and broadcast news of it before most Egyptians had heard about it. Since everyone inside Egypt and abroad had already heard about the incident, and it looked as if there was government neglect involved, the government had to release a few statements about it and even find one or two people upon whom to pin the blame. Things being that way, the

Egyptian media had no alternative but to take an interest in what happened.

Thus, the newspapers and magazines filled their pages with the precise details of the accident, without exercising their usual caution not to assign blame to any government heavyweights for their dereliction of duty. Suddenly there were completely frank features about that large and neglected portion of the Egyptian populace, how its members live, how they travel from place to place, the kind of work they do in Cairo, how much they earn in wages, how the government treats them on the train and off, what services they expect to get from the government and what they have despaired of getting. And so on.

The truth is that, despite the grisly nature of the accident and the huge number of victims, it is not at all strange that something like this might have happened. What may seem strange is that it does not happen more often. In all honesty, accidents arising from similar causes do happen in Egypt every day. What made the one that occurred on February 19, 2002, unique was not the type of accident, but the number of its victims. In fact, reading the details printed about it and its related incidents, the stories of those who escaped, and what those who had lost relatives in the fire had to say, one gains a startlingly precise and comprehensive description of many aspects of Egyptian society today. That is what I shall attempt to elucidate here.

Train number 832, which leaves Cairo station every evening at 11:30, bound for Aswan on a sixteen-hour trip was, on that day, the eve of the Feast of the Sacrifice, made up of fourteen passenger cars—nine third-class and five second-class—two luggage cars, an engine and a caboose.

Each third-class car had seating for ninety-six passengers, but on that night the cars carried more than double that number, seating passengers three or four to a seat, in the aisles between the seats, in the luggage racks over the seats, and in the passageways between the cars. The windows were blocked completely so no one could jump out and escape, either from the conductor if a passenger happened to board without a ticket or, as it happened, from a fire. The truth is that Egyptian National Railways had received the trains from European factories equipped with windows that open and close but had added fixed iron bars to them to prevent people leaving through them. The passengers themselves had further stuffed them up with cardboard, blankets, and even articles of clothing to replace the glass that had with time been broken and never replaced. On cold nights, like those in February, passengers needed something to shut out the wind. Most of the doors were locked shut for some reason or another, or they could only be opened with great difficulty. Even if they could be opened, they were blocked by the kind of people who were well known to the regular passengers as thugs, who would set up stands between the seats and the doors, selling drinks that looked like lemonade, and at exorbitant prices. They would intimidate the passengers into buying the drinks and threaten them if they refused, or make taking a seat conditional upon buying a drink. All of this was done by agreement with the conductors, the train inspectors and the police, so it did no good to complain.

One can imagine the sight of the third-class cars when the train blew its whistle to depart. Crowds of people piled one on top of the other on the seats, in the aisles, in the luggage racks, all huddling together against the cold, the passengers on one side and the thugs on the other. The only thing that made the journey at all bearable for the passengers was the thought of meeting their relatives upon arrival in Minya, Edfu, Sohag, or Aswan, and spending the vacation with them, and imagining the looks on their children's faces when they saw the presents they had brought with them from Cairo.

The five cars of the second class, called "regular second class" to distinguish them from "special second class," which is not available on that type of train, are not much better than the third class except in a few respects. They are slightly less crowded and the thugs are not quite as conspicuous. But the two classes share other important qualities. One of those is that there is no way of communicating with the driver, who does not feel any connection or obligation to the passengers, but simply carries out the orders coming to him from his immediate superior. It is not his business to know anything about the passengers' state of affairs or their needs, even in a life or death situation. There is no mirror by which he can see the cars behind him, nor any communication device—not even an antique one—connecting the engine to the caboose. The emergency brake cable is either out of commission or was never present in the first place, and thus there is no warning signal that a passenger might use to alert the driver of any dangerous occurrence. The whole picture looks very much like the relation (or rather the lack of it) between the Egyptian government and the lower classes in Egypt (whose members ride the third class carriages on any train) or the lower middle class (whose members ride the regular second class). The upper classes do not even ride such trains; if they wish to travel to Upper Egypt, they either fly or take an entirely different kind of train, one with functioning windows and doors, air conditioning, and dining cars; a train like that has many safety devices and is subject to the best-quality maintenance. When it was announced, for example, that the deputy minister of industry had been among the victims of the disaster, many people were shocked to think that there might be a deputy of any ministry on such a train. That mistake was soon corrected in a prominent place in *Al-Ahram* newspaper, however, as it appeared that there had indeed been a victim in the hospital with exactly the same name as, but bearing no other relationship whatsoever to, the deputy minister of industry.

At 1:15 in the morning the incident occurred. Some survivors thought that the blaze was started by an electrical short in the last car of the train, as they remembered noticing a burning smell from the point when the train left Cairo; others thought that a kerosene stove near the door of car number eleven may have exploded, according to the technical report filed with the prosecutor's office.

160

Whatever the case, an electrical short or a flaring stove turned into a great blaze, spreading rapidly from suitcase to seat to passenger, and from one third-class car to another with astonishing speed owing to the density of the passengers piled one on top of the other. Some tried to jump out of the windows, but they could not because of the iron bars. One passenger reportedly succeeded in getting his child through the bars, throwing him from the train, in the hope that he himself would jump out of the door, but he could not reach it. The fire engulfed seven cars, allowing none to escape save a few vigorous youths, who were closest to the doors and managed to open them or break them down and then fling themselves from the train, which was traveling faster than one hundred kilometers per hour. Some of them fell into the fields, sustaining various injuries and lying unconscious until the morning, when they were found by farm workers. Others fell into the irrigation ditch, eighteen of whom were later found drowned. But some escaped, either to die later, or to relate in hysterical tones what they had seen.

When the whole thing was over, it emerged that the driver did not know that the train had caught fire until the train had traveled another eighteen kilometers from the point where the fire broke out. He related that he only learned of it when the train reached the Abu 'Ammar curve, which allowed the driver's assistant to have a look back at the cars. But it is also said that the way he learned that his train was on fire was from the driver of another train passing in the opposite direction. That is when he stopped and he and his assistant uncoupled the burning cars from the rest and continued on to Aswan with the second-class carriages and the two surviving ones from the third class. Meanwhile, the fire engines and rescue vehicles were of no use since by the time they arrived, everything organic and inorganic had been turned into cinders.

By reading what was published about the victims, their identities, their hometowns and villages, and the work they performed in Cairo, we can gain a glimpse of the living conditions of the lower classes in Egypt today. All were going home to spend a short vacation with their families. Some of them were students from less prestigious faculties that do not require high grades or too much spending on private tutoring. Some were low-level employees in the government or some company or another. But most of them were laborers, described variously by their surviving relatives as spot laborers, peddlers, doormen, and the like. More important than this is the number of dependents they were supporting in Upper Egypt. Regardless of the low wages they were earning in Cairo, some were supporting a wife and four or more children. Others were supporting two aging parents and numerous unemployed brothers and sisters. Still others were supporting all of those, wives, children, parents, and siblings. Thus the disaster did not just bring emotional distress to the relatives of the victims, but financial calamity as well. There was also a significant number of passengers who were unemployed, who could not find work in their own locales in Upper Egypt, and had been similarly unsuccessful in finding work in Cairo; now they were returning home empty-handed.

The whole picture also sums up the kind of relationship that has grown up over the years between Cairo and Upper Egypt. A capital city, as oppressive as its name in Arabic suggests *(al-Qahira)*[17], dispatches trains every day to the south to return with thousands of people looking for work or a chance to study, but in fact gives them jobs no better than those jobs that oblige them to cram themselves onto trains of this type, and arouses in them no greater hope than that they might simply enjoy seeing their loved ones for a few days during the vacation.

If this is the way things are, what then was the purpose of all those investments, loans, and growth rates, high or low? What of all this talk about modernization, the "social dimension of economic policy," and the interests of low-income groups? What use was all the talk about the right exchange rate against the dollar, if the result, with or without high growth rates, or high or low dollar values, is an economy which continues to run trains of this type and with the same degree of misery for its passengers, year after year?

If one puts all that aside and concentrates on what happened to the victims *after* the incident, one must note first the large number of families who came from Upper Egypt searching for news of their loved ones. They knew for certain that they had been on the train, but they had not seen any trace of them. They first looked for them in the hospitals hoping against hope that they might only be injured. Not finding them there, they looked for their names or descriptions in the lists the police and rescue workers were able to construct. From there, in utter despair, to the morgue in a last attempt to find anything recognizable among the corpses. No luck there either.

The compression of human bodies had been so great in those seven cars, and the time it took for the driver to discover the fire had been so long that the bodies had been burned to charred fragments, with no way of recognizing faces or any other distinguishing features or the clothing they were wearing on the day they died. Any peculiar marks of individuality had been obliterated. The passengers had been transformed into a single black lump, not much different in death than they had been regarded in life: a single undifferentiated human mass. It was as if the fire, knowing how they had been treated in life, treated them just the same in death. The only thing new was that now even their families could not tell them apart.

This appalling carbonization of the passengers allowed the authorities to set the number of dead at whatever they liked. So they fixed the number at 375, as if this were a sure figure, even though it was impossible in the circumstances to assign any number with confidence; the number of victims must have been much higher than that. Each of the seven cars that burned was equipped to hold around one hundred. According to those who escaped, they were filled with more than double that number. This would make the number of passengers closer to two thousand than to three or four hundred. The workers at the nearest hospital said that they were unable to receive more than 350 of the injured, and they transferred the rest to other hospitals. These were the ones who had managed to throw themselves from the train. Others had died of the impact when hitting the ground, or of drowning in the irrigation canal, or from being hit by an oncoming train as they lay unconscious on the tracks where they fell. Thus perhaps no more than five hundred managed to escape from the train, but these cannot possibly represent most of the passengers of those seven cars for the reasons already mentioned.

Of the bodies of the victims, 195 were identified and their names and those of the towns and villages from which they came were published. The great majority, as might be expected, were men, and most were no older than thirty years of age. Not a single one of their names appeared in the obituaries of the newspaper _Al-Ahram_ as do the names of the deceased of other classes. The victims, both known and unknown, were buried together in a mass grave in the hope that people might forget the incident in the shortest time possible. To make sure of that, even the place for the funerary prayer was changed at the last minute, after thousands had gathered for the service.

This mass grave, however, posed a difficult problem. The Muslim families of the deceased could never conceive that their lost loved ones might be buried without the proper Islamic ablutions to prepare the dead for the grave. They would neither rest nor sleep until they made sure that the rites had been properly performed. To forgo them would be to inspire a sense of grief and anger that was even greater than that caused by the death in the first place. What could the authorities do? They thought of a ploy (and do they ever fail to think up some ploy?). They gained a religious legal decree from the Sheikh of al-Azhar mosque that the victims should be considered martyrs. According to Islamic law, the body of a martyr need not be washed before burial.

This solution offered relief to the families of the departed respecting their final resting place, but what about the other, more worldly problem of the financial situation of those families after the death of their loved ones, their only means of support? The government decreed three thousand pounds in compensation for each of the families of the victims, and a Saudi prince donated even more than that. But compensation required positive proof of death, otherwise opportunistic con men might have attempted to take advantage of the situation and collect money that they did not deserve. The authorities, as we have come to expect from them, take greater precautions to guard themselves against potential cheats than against anything else. So they required of the families that they identify the bodies of their lost loved ones, or at least provide documentation that they were on the train that night and that they did not leap off it or manage to be rescued in some way or another. Then they had to prove their degree of relationship to the deceased, and if they could not present positive proof of death, they should at least prove that they were missing. That, however, required a court petition and the decision of a judge, and only after the passage of four years from the time of the alleged disappearance. In either case, death or disappearance, the families had to prove that the deceased had not taken out life insurance that would exceed the amount of compensation being offered by the government. It is unlikely that third-class passengers would think of life insurance, but prudence dictates such precautions. Taking all this into consideration, it must have seemed to many of the relatives of the victims that death itself may be easier and more merciful than meeting the conditions for compensation.

Be that as it may, all of these conditions and complications throw some light on the behavior of some of the families, who rushed to identify the bodies of their dead by any superficial resemblance between them and what they discovered in the remains, alleging, for example, that this shred of clothing or that shoe was what they were wearing when they died, or that a platinum pin emerging from some part of a corpse identified a certain person because before he died he had surgery to insert just such a pin. And so it went. But getting the financial compensation was not always the reason for such haste. One of the relatives said that he had rushed to identify his brother's body to please his aged father who refused to return to the village until his son's remains were found. In such a confused and chaotic situation many strange things could happen, for example, a family claimed the body of their lost loved one and took it home for burial, only to find later that there was a person of the same name still among the living in a hospital in a remote town.

Such incidents, however, must have been rare. The great majority of families would have returned to their towns and villages having lost hope of finding their loved ones, alive or dead. As far as I can see, the only thing that enables them to carry on with life, in spite of everything, is that nothing in their previous experience would have led them to expect any better treatment.

# 14

## The Doctorate

I wish someone would collect some figures from newspapers, magazines, the radio, and television to see how many people on the news hold doctorates. Whoever did would find that their absolute number as well as their proportion of the total number of writers, expert consultants, commentators, cabinet ministers, and other persons of authority are greater in Egypt than in many other countries, developed or otherwise. The phenomenon bears scrutiny since it is not to be welcomed without some serious reservations. It also reveals some unfortunate truths about the state of Egyptian society today.

There is, first of all, the simple truth that not everyone who is highly learned is able to impart that learning to others. The mass media, by addressing such a wide audience, obviously requires a style of speaking or writing different from that required in the lecture hall or in the writing of a technical text. The fact is, however, that many Ph.D.s who appear repeatedly in the Egyptian media do not possess the right qualities for reaching the audience, regardless of how well-informed they may be. As a result, the discussions in newspapers and in the broadcast media are replete with runic incantations about such things as the Egyptian economic crisis, the effects of globalization, or the origin of postmodernism, that must leave the poor audience utterly confused.

Even worse than that, many of these authors and commentators with Ph.D.s are often aware of the true effect of what they say or write, and instead of bowing out gracefully, exploit the situation to their own benefit at the expense of their readers and listeners. Many of them can fill an entire page of a newspaper with seemingly profound compositions, without expressing a single lucid thought. On they go, repeating things that have been said a hundred times before or reiterating the contents of first-year textbooks of the disciplines in which they received their doctoral degrees. Or they recite well-worn, self-evident platitudes, but in obscure language, relying on the impossibility of anyone other than a specialist in the field understanding them, and sprinkling their essays with unfamiliar technical terms, when they might have made things so much easier with the addition of a simple word here and there. Many of them do all of this intentionally, otherwise they would be exposed, and readers would see plainly that there is nothing to what they are saying, or that it is well known to everyone, or that it is not true in the first place.

In such a predicament, affixing the title of "Dr." to the author's name is an effective means of concealing the vacuity of the essay's content. Indeed, it may be the only way possible of getting it published, since readers (perhaps even the editor-in-chief) may think that words such as these coming from the holder of a doctoral degree could not possibly be mere trivialities. Any perceived shortcoming must be on the part of the readers, who are unable to understand what they read either because of their lack of intelligence or the dearth of their knowledge.

There are many other ways of gulling the readers. Instead of using so many difficult and poorly-translated terms, why not simply insert the term as it is, in foreign script or transliterated into Arabic? Why not drop in the names of foreign writers whom readers will not have heard of before, or refer to recently published books that the reader has no hope of obtaining? Even better, why not cite conference proceedings, mentioning that the conference was attended by the best and brightest (implying of course that the writer of the essay is one of them)?

The phenomenon can also be seen in cabinet ministers and others in top government positions. In fact, it has become rare to find a minister or prime minister who does not hold a doctoral degree, and the phenomenon has spread from such ministries as those of economy, planning, and finance, where one might think that holding a doctorate may be useful, to such positions as the minister of supply or of religious endowments. It is very unlikely that this has contributed to better job performance, since ministerial positions demand skills and abilities not remotely related to those required for scholarly success.

If anything like this exists anywhere else in the East or the West, I am unaware of it. I am not even aware of anything like it in any other Arab country. From what I know of the countries of the world, holding a doctoral degree does not open doors nearly as easily as it does in Egypt; but even in Egypt this phenomenon is a relatively new one. Before the middle of the twentieth century, it was rare to find a minister who held a Ph.D.—many distinguished ministers at the time, even in ministries that are less political in nature, such as those of education, labor, or health, did not. In the arts and media too, during the first half of the century, the great majority of Egypt's leading men of letters had not earned doctoral degrees, and none of them seemed to have felt an urgent need to have one. Those who did have doctorates avoided making an issue out of the fact, confident in the knowledge that their status did not depend on it. They even felt that it was a little dishonest to use the title when writing about something that did not relate to the fields of study in which they had earned their degrees, lest readers mistakenly assume that the writers had a special expertise in the field about which they were writing.

How can one explain this change? The first thing that springs to mind, of course, is the unprecedented rise in doctoral degrees over the last forty or fifty years, a result partly of the spread of university education, and partly of the tendency of universities, over time, to make it easier to earn doctorates. In addition, there was the expansion of government-sponsored scholarships for study abroad, which continued until the end of the 1960s, as well as the increase in the number of fellowships offered by European and American institutions in the succeeding years.

But this is not very useful, for it fails to explain the readiness to appoint Ph.D. holders to jobs for which they were otherwise unprepared, like the jobs of cabinet ministers or of writers or broadcasters in the media. I can think of two other possible explanations, one relating to the ministers and the other to the media.

The first relates to the disruption of the old political order based on party politics that came about as a result of the revolution. Prior to 1952, the nomination of ministers was the preserve of the party in power, and only candidates who had proved their loyalty to the party and who were active in its affairs were appointed. This, of course, did not require a Ph.D. When the revolution came along, all political parties were disbanded. This created a huge void, which was hard to fill. The easiest solution and the closest to hand was to appoint military officers to the ministries and positions of authority, which was justified by the conditions of the revolution. Nevertheless, the running of some ministries, such as those of economy, finance, education, health, justice, and culture required skills and qualifications not readily found among military officers.

There were not many among the leadership of the revolution, or among their associates, who could take these on. So it must have been natural to think of university professors, on the assumption that professors, by virtue of their qualifications, must have knowledge of the requisite fields, and so the necessary ability to direct a technical ministry, and that there must exist at least some university professors must believe in the goals of the revolution.

In the 1970s, there was another reason for the increase in demand for Ph.D. holders, for the revolution, which had been at full power throughout the 1950s and 1960s, began to wither and fade after the Israeli attack of 1967 and even more after the death of Gamal 'Abd al-Nasser in 1970. After that, loyalty to the principles of the revolution was not a sufficient justification for ascending to the top posts. Indeed, it might even have lessened the chances of promotion. The function of ministers and other authorities was transformed from a political to a purely technocratic one, and people of no political stripe (and hence no particular loyalty or affiliation) whatsoever came into demand. But since candidates had no political identity to distinguish them one from another, the title of doctor would help to render them more attractive, at least when their appointment was announced to the public.

This may go part of the way toward explaining the spread of Ph.D. holders in the press and mass media as well. But there is probably another more important factor, for it is important to distinguish between the readership of the newspapers and magazines, and even the radio audiences of the 1940s and 1950s, and those of the 1980s and 1990s. We must not forget how small the number of educated college graduates was fifty years ago compared to their number today. Nor should we forget the differences in the quality of their education. The newspaper and magazine readers and the radio audience of fifty or sixty years ago were generally more sophisticated and demanding, possessing greater powers of discernment in matters of style and content. As a result, it must be much easier for a low quality writer to hold a secure position in newspapers, magazines, and radio (and now television too) today than it was fifty years ago. That being so, the title of doctor can serve as a ruse to trick the readers or audiences, and even the press and media authorities themselves, to a degree greater than it could in the past.

When the word got out that holding a doctorate would open doors, bringing no mean monetary reward, status, and fame, regardless of the real abilities of the holder, everyone wanted to have one. Some even go as far as to place the title next to their names without having really earned the degree, relying on people's gullibility, and may even go so far as to believe that continually putting the title next to their name may ultimately cause the lie to become a reality.

# 15

## This World and the Next

In this last chapter I will relate a more personal story, about a change that has occurred in my own family over four generations—those of my grandfather, my father, myself, and my son. The story revolves around one single theme, namely our changing view of this world as compared with the next.

In my father's autobiography, published in Arabic some fifty years ago (Ahmad Amin, *My Life*, Cairo, 1950) this description of my grandfather's character appears, revealing his view on this matter:

> He is an exceedingly religious man, prays frequently and reads the Qur'an and Prophetic Traditions avidly. He distributes alms among his

177

poorer relatives, fasts, performs the Pilgrimage, and stands at night in prayer, singing the praises of Allah. If he commits any evil, or what he regards as evil, he is profuse in his remorse and repentance. Abstemious in his pursuit of material gain, except insofar as it meets the needs of his family; if he puts anything aside, it is against any future need. Constant in his remembrance of mortality, he has memorized Prophetic sayings about the futility of the world, the pettiness of its concerns, and its insignificance next to Allah. He has built his tomb, which he visits often, there to recite the Qur'an, in the hope that this will make it a blessed place of repose for himself at his death. He scorns the adornments and joys of this world. One time I saw him in his room hesitating over dressing for an official occasion; suddenly he stepped out of his fancy suit, threw it into the corner, saying, 'the life of this world is no more than play and adornment.' Whereupon he sat reciting the Qur'an. He is simple in his food and drink, his clothing and his sleep, so that he eats what is put before him contentedly, he sleeps on a simple straw mat, and dresses neatly in simple clothing without any foppery. His world consists of his Azhar, the mosque, his books, and the people of his neighborhood. Of the political, economic, or social concerns that his neighbors chase after, he has no knowledge. He never reads the papers, unless one falls into his hand by accident, and he never sits around with people discussing the concerns of the day.

This was a man whose religion filled his life. Indeed, religion for him was a matter of personal salvation; in his mind, it had nothing to do with political or social issues or with the goal of national revival, of which he was aware, but with which he did not occupy his mind. To him the state of the nation was the same at his birth as it would be at his death. In any case, his own hopes for his nation were hardly relevant, for there was nothing he could do to bring them about; if they were to happen, they would happen when Allah so willed.

My father was also without doubt a religious man. But his view of the world and religion were very different from that of my grandfather. For him personal redemption was no doubt important, but what was more important was the redemption of the nation. He thought all the time about ways of reforming the nation and the causes of his country's backwardness, when other nations had advanced along the path of progress. When he was married, he recorded his feelings of the day on the back of his wedding photograph, ending with the words, "I pray Allah that he ordain for me some great work by which I might serve my nation socially and morally." When he was a student at school, he was asked to prepare a speech to present to the assembled students, teachers, and guests. He chose as his theme, "The reasons for Muslim weakness," which he ascribed to two causes: corruption in government and "that men of religion take the side of and endorse corrupt governments by fostering in the hearts of the people a resigned acceptance of fate and comfort in the afterlife, while denying them any comfort in this life."

This obsessive concern for national revival was the main difference between my father's view of the place of religion in the world and my grandfather's. But there was an important thing binding them together: the nation whose rebirth so consumed my father was the Muslim nation, of which my grandfather also felt himself to be a part.

When my father wrote his book *Modern Leaders of Reform* (Cairo, 1948), he did not confine himself just to Egyptian or Arab leaders. He included Turkish and Indian Muslim leaders as well, all of whom, in my father's view, had one goal, namely the reform of Muslims and the rebirth of the Islamic nation. Although he did show loyalty to the cause of Egyptian and Arab advancement and Arab unity, he continued, until his death in the mid-1950s, to view both issues as two aspects of the larger and more important issue of a Muslim renaissance. He took the greatest interest in the revolution of Kemal Ataturk in Turkey, for example, viewing the decisions taken by Ataturk in light of the degree of their applicability outside of Turkey. In my father's view, Turkey was a part of the same "nation" to which he belonged. This was my grandfather's view too, but, if anyone ever brought to my grandfather's attention what was happening there, he was not ready to accept any talk about reinterpreting religion in the

180

name of social or political reform. My father, on the other hand, was ready to listen to such talk, discuss it, and accept some of it.

This difference in outlook of position between my father and grandfather with regard to the place of religion in the world was not strange or hard to interpret. For let us compare the way my grandfather was raised and educated with that of my father. My grandfather was born just before the middle of the nineteenth century, in a political and cultural climate which fostered the belief that the larger entity to which one belonged was neither the Egyptian state nor the Arab world, but the Islamic nation or *umma*. The concept of a nation state was indeed unfamiliar to Egyptians and Arabs until my grandfather reached at least the age of forty. The idea took root in Egypt in the last quarter of the nineteenth century and did not come into full bloom until after the First World War. The education my grandfather received was an Azhari one, and no other, and his world did not extend beyond Cairo; indeed he knew no more of Cairo than the neighborhoods around al-Azhar mosque and Giza.

My father, on the other hand, was endowed with a great deal more practical and theoretical knowledge. He was born five years after the 'Urabi revolt of 1881, and saw the soldiers of the British occupation when he was a small child. The Dinshaway incident occurred when he was twenty; he read in the papers about the sentencing of four of villagers to death and others to flogging and imprisonment for the death of one British officer who had gone to the village to shoot pigeons, although it was never certain whether he died from the blow of a stick wielded by one of the villagers or of sunstroke. My father and his friends wept bitterly when they read of the sentence. He himself later learned English and read works in the English language, not just about Islamic history but also about philosophy, literature, and history. While it is true that he felt miserable when he first boarded a train for Tanta, only 100 kilometers from Cairo, at leaving his family for the first time at the age of sixteen, he nevertheless later traveled to Turkey, Lebanon, Syria, and even to some European countries, even though this all happened after he had turned fifty.

Thus, my father's experience of the world was quite wide, when compared with that of my grandfather. His devotion to his religion was deep, but it coexisted with his interest in this world. In spite of being religious he did not belittle money and worldly success, and the issue of national revival in this world occupied him as much as did matters of recompense and requital for the next. In an essay he entitled "A Friend," he was really describing himself when he said "in his mind he reconciled contradictions and resolved paradoxes. He combined the way of the religious with belief in the theory of survival of the fittest, as well as belief in determinism with a belief in free choice. He collected in his library ancient books, worm-eaten, and woven in the weft of time, as well as the shiniest new books of European thought. He kept as friends drunks and ascetics, the dissolute and the devout."

* * *

Then I came along. I did not go to a Qur'anic school or to al-Azhar. Instead, I went to a modern school in Heliopolis to learn English alongside Arabic and the rudiments of French. My father had not been convinced with the old style of schooling prevalent in Egypt at the time, so he sent me to the model school which he had heard used the most modern and up-to-date techniques of education. Religion was not the crux of my reading and thought as it had been for my father when he was younger and for my grandfather throughout his entire life. Instead, it was taught to us in a religion class, alongside history, geography, and music classes, the substance of which was entirely secular.

As the realm of religion around me shrank, the realm of the world widened. The newspapers and magazines that my grandfather did not even look at and that my father, as a young man, would buy only on special occasions, came regularly to our house without anyone having to send for them. The cinema, which had not even been invented when my grandfather was fifty, and which my father had never entered until he himself was fifty, and which he only went to once or twice in his whole life, I first went to when I was five or six, and used regularly as a means of entertainment. Airplanes, which up until my grandfather died had only been used in war, and which my father never boarded until he was sixty, I first boarded at the age of fifteen.

My grandfather thought that he could do nothing of any significance for the sake of reform, while my father thought that reform was possible, if difficult to achieve, that which was called for being reform of the Muslims. As for me, my own belief in reform was stronger than that of my father in his youth, and in my eyes that meant reform for Egypt and the Arabs. The political sustenance to be found at the time when I became politically aware was the usual Egyptian diet, involving removing the English from Egypt, reform of the Egyptian political system, and social justice between rich and poor Egyptians. The news reaching us from other Arab countries was sporadic, without any sense of urgency. This changed somewhat after the partition of Palestine in 1947 and the outbreak of the war for Palestine. I was twelve at the time. The revolution of 1952 refocused our attention for a few years on purely Egyptian issues, but when the Egyptian regime began to emphasize ties with the Arab world and the problem of Palestine after the mid-1950s, the concern for reform expanded somewhat to include reform for the whole Arab nation. By that time I had turned twenty. The condition of Egypt, then, took precedence for me, and the concept of reform of the Muslim world was much further away. It did not animate me the way it had my father.

I had moved far away from the standpoint that my father reached, to say nothing of that of my grandfather, but my son, who is now thirty, has reached an outlook far removed from all of those that the three generations preceding him had possessed. When it came time for him to begin school, the government schools had already reached an advanced state of decline. This made me prefer to place him in one of the so-called "language schools." This name was applied to those schools whose main language of instruction was English or French. Nationalized by the government in the 1950s, they were left with some degree of independence in certain issues, among them the teaching of some subjects in English, and an emphasis on sports and social activities more than that of other schools. My father had likened the effect of his learning a foreign language to that of allowing a person to see the world with two pairs of eyes rather than one. He began learning English when he was almost thirty years old. What about my son, who was better than either my father or myself at reading English when he was only ten? To my father, the cinema was a marvel. To me it was a form of entertainment to be resorted to from time to time, and only rarely did I as a boy and a young man see a film that was not Egyptian. But for my son, the cinema has become almost a necessity of life, whereby he watches Egyptian, American, Indian, and Italian films. It is difficult for him to imagine life without it. As for the television, which had not appeared in Egypt by the time my father died, and did not come to our house until I had passed thirty, by the age of six my son was watching the comic play, "School for Troublemakers," which ridiculed the very idea of education and reform.

My grandfather thought reform was impossible. My father thought it was possible, and the reform of Muslims highly desirable. I too saw it as possible, but I was thinking mainly of Egypt. I see my son behaving and hear him talking as if reform is highly unlikely either for the

Muslims, the Arabs, or for Egypt. He often acts as if the best thing is to mind one's own business. He does not trouble his mind with things over which he feels he has very little influence. The most one can do, he seems to think, is to work for small and incremental change, which is the only way one might gain some small influence on things. My son seems at first sight to have returned to the same point from which my grandfather began, in his belief that one cannot effect any significant change in society, much less the whole universe. But there is a great difference between the origin of that point of view for my grandfather and for my son. My grandfather arrived at that point through his reading of religious books; my son arrived at it by acquainting himself with such things as history and politics and by hearing the news of the world on television. Surprisingly, the result is very much the same.

# Notes

1. A low-market weekly newspaper.
2. A junior member of the Muslim Brotherhood, imprisoned and later executed by the Nasser administration in August 1966, Sayed Qutb's writings have been inspirational to later generations of Muslim radicals.
3. An enormously popular television preacher, whose theology continues to be widely accepted even after his death.
4. Some of the genuine luminaries of Egypt's early twentieth century writers, 'Abbas al-'Aqqad was a political and social reformer, poet, literary critic, and essayist; Tawfīk al-Hakim, a playwright and novelist; and Salama Musa a polymath philosopher and scientific thinker.
5. Three of the most prominent Egyptian writers of the late twentieth century in Egypt—Idris, mostly famous for his short stories; Awad, a social historian and critic; and Mahfouz, a novelist and winner of the Nobel prize for literature in 1988.
6. The founders and editors of *Akhbar al-Yawm.*
7. The Wahhabis are a fundamentalist sect of Islam known for their extreme and austere views.
8. A wimple-like garment covering the hair and neck that is thought to satisfy the Islamic prescription for veiling.
9. Which is to say, he had been educated at al-Azhar

university. Founded in CE 971, it is the oldest university in the world and has remained a seat of Islamic education to this day.

10. Often known in the west as the "fez" after the city of that name in Morocco where a similar piece of headgear was also manufactured.

11. A piaster is one one-hundredth of an Egyptian pound.

12. Purists maintain that women should cover their hair completely, wear clothing that does not reveal the contours of the body, and eschew wearing makeup.

13. The seventh day of life has been celebrated since ancient times in Egypt and involves a specific set of rituals, still observed.

14. Sa'id is the son of Muhammad 'Ali, who ruled from 1854–63, and granted the concession for digging the Suez Canal. Ismail is Mohamed Ali's grandson, who ruled Egypt between 1863 and 1879 when, under British and French pressure, he was deposed by the Ottoman sultan.

15. I have dealt in some detail with the impact of these two factors, foreign pressure and corruption, on Egypt's economic development in my book, *Egypt's Economic Predicament: A Study in the Interaction of External Pressure, Political Folly and Social Tension in Egypt, 1960-1990* (Brill, Leiden, 1995).

16. The reference is to the novel *Sybil,* in which Disraeli describes England as "two nations between whom there is no intercourse and sympathy; who are igno-

rant of each other's habits, thoughts, and feelings, as if they were dwellers in different zones or inhabitants of different planets."

17. The Arabic name for Cairo, *al-Qahira*, suggests two meanings: 'the Victorious' and 'the Oppressive.'